Colonial America Biographies

Colonial America Biographies

Volume 1:
A-L

PEGGY SAARI
Julie Carnagie, Editor

AN IMPRINT OF THE GALE GROUP

DETROIT · SAN FRANCISCO · LONDON
BOSTON · WOODBRIDGE, CT

Colonial America: Biographies

Peggy Saari

Staff

Julie L. Carnagie, *U•X•L Editor*
Carol DeKane Nagel, *U•X•L Managing Editor*
Thomas L. Romig, *U•X•L Publisher*

Shalice Shah-Caldwell, *Permissions Associate (Pictures)*

Rita Wimberley, *Senior Buyer*
Evi Seoud, *Assistant Production Manager*
Dorothy Maki, *Manufacturing Manager*

Pamela A. E. Galbreath, *Senior Art Director*
Cynthia Baldwin, *Product Design Manager*

LM Design, *Typesetting*

Library of Congress Cataloging-in-Publication Data

Saari, Peggy.
   Colonial America : biographies / Peggy Saari : Julie L. Carnagie, editor.
      p.   cm.
   Includes bibliographical references and indexes.
      Contents: v. 1. A-L — v. 2. M-Z.
   Summary: Profiles sixty men and women from the American colonial era, including explorers, founders of colonies, religious leaders, landowners, artists, and more.
   ISBN 0-7876-3760-2 (set). — ISBN   0-7876-3761-0 (v. 1). — ISBN 0-7876-3762-9 (v. 2)
   1. United States—History—Colonial period, ca. 1600-1775 Biography Dictionaries Juvenile literature. [1. United   States—History—Colonial period, ca. 1600-1775 Biography.] I. Carnagie, Julie. II. Title.
   E187.5.S23   1999
   973.2'092'2
   [B]—DC21   99-20707
                                                                                       CIP

Cover photographs (top to bottom): Cotton Mather reproduced by permission of the Library of Congress; Anne Marbury Hutchinson reproduced by permission Corbis Corporation (Bellevue); Pontiac reproduced by permission of the city of Pontiac, Michigan.

Printed in the United States of America

10 9 8 7 6 5 4 3

47 50

Contents

Volume 2: M-Z

Advisory Board

Special thanks are due for the invaluable comments and suggestions provided by U•X•L's Colonial America Reference Library advisors:

- Katherine L. Bailey, Library Media Specialist, Seabreeze High School, Daytona Beach, Florida.

- Jonathan Betz-Zall, Children's Librarian, Sno-Isle Regional Library System, Edmonds, Washington.

- Deborah Hammer, Manager of the Social Sciences Division, Queens Borough Public Library, New Hyde Park, New York.

- Fannie Louden, Fifth Grade History Teacher, B. F. Yancey Elementary School, Esmont, Virginia.

Reader's Guide

Colonial America: Biographies presents the biographies of women and men relevant to the colonial era in America. Among the sixty people profiled in each of the two volumes are explorers, Native Americans, and people who helped to found and shape the American colonies. *Colonial America: Biographies* does not only include biographies of readily recognizable figures of the colonial era, such as Italian explorer Christopher Columbus, founder of the Pennsylvania colony William Penn, and banished religious leader Anne Marbury Hutchinson, but it also includes profiles of people such as Margaret Brent, the first woman landowner in Maryland, and John Smibert, the first painter to capture life in the colonies.

Additional features

Colonial America: Biographies also contains short biographies of people who are in some way connected with the main biographee and sidebars highlighting interesting information. More than one hundred black-and-white illustrations enliven the text, while cross-references are made to other people profiled in the two-volume set. Each entry concludes with a list of sources—including web sites—for further information for additional study, and both volumes contain a timeline, a glossary, and a cumulative index of the subjects discussed in *Colonial America: Biographies.*

Comments and suggestions

We welcome your comments on this work as well as your suggestions for topics to be featured in future editions of *Colonial America: Biographies.* Please write: Editors, *Colonial America: Biographies,* U•X•L, 27500 Drake Rd., Farmington Hills, MI 48331-3535; call toll-free: 1-800-877-4253; fax: 248-414-5043; or send e-mail via www.galegroup.com.

Timeline of Events in Colonial America

1492   Italian explorer **Christopher Columbus** opens the way for European settlement of the Americas.

1524   Italian explorer **Giovanni da Verrazano** becomes the first European to sight New York Harbor.

1535   French explorer **Jacques Cartier** discovers the St. Lawrence River.

1538   Spanish conquistador **Francisco Vásquez de Coronado** begins searching for the fabled Seven Cities of Cibola.

1539   Moroccan "medicine man" **Estevanico** is killed by Zuni warriors.

1542   Spanish explorer **Hernando de Soto** leads the first European party to discover the Mississippi River.

1495-97	1517	1534
Leonardo da Vinci paints *The Last Supper*	Martin Luther posts his 95 theses	Henry VIII founds Church of England

| 1475 | 1500 | 1525 | 1550 |

1608	Powhatan-Renapé "princess" **Pocahontas** saves Jamestown settlers from starvation.
1609	English navigator **Henry Hudson** discovers the Hudson River, a major waterway in present-day New York State.
1609	Chief **Powhatan** establishes peaceful relations with the Virginia colonists.
1612	French explorer **Samuel de Champlain** founds New France.
1612	Virginia colonist **John Rolfe** perfects a strain of tobacco for export to England.
1614	Former Virginia colonist **John Smith** explores and names New England.
1621	Wampanoag chief **Massasoit** signs a treaty with the Plymouth colonists.
1627	Massachusetts fur trader **Thomas Morton** angers Puritans by building a giant Maypole and celebrating May Day.
1630	Plymouth Colony governor **William Bradford** begins writing *Of Plymouth Plantation.*
1630	Puritan leader **John Winthrop** founds Massachusetts Bay Colony.
1633	Influential Puritan clergyman **John Cotton** moves to the Massachusetts Bay Colony.
1636	Massachusetts Bay Colony leader **John Endecott** initiates the Pequot War.
1638	Religious dissenter **Anne Marbury Hutchinson** is put on trial for heresy.
1639	French missionary **Marie Guyart** moves to New France to start a convent for Native Americans.

1616	1620	1625		1636
William Shakespeare dies	The Mayflower Compact is signed	Fort Amsterdam is founded	1633 Galileo is tried for heresy	Harvard College is founded

| 1610 | 1620 | 1630 | 1640 |

1644 Religious and political dissident **Roger Williams** founds Rhode Island.

1646 Dutch military leader **Peter Stuyvesant** is appointed director-general of New Netherlands.

c. 1647 Amateur lawyer **Margaret Brent** unsuccessfully petitions the Maryland assembly for the right to vote.

1650 *The Tenth Muse,* a collection of poems by Massachusetts Puritan poet **Anne Bradstreet,** is published. She is America's first female poet.

1651 Former African slave **Anthony Johnson** owns a 250-acre estate at Pungoteague Creek in Virginia.

1651 Puritan preacher and educator **John Eliot** establishes the first town for "praying Indians."

1660 Quaker dissident **Mary Dyer** is executed by Puritans in Massachusetts.

1670s Puritan minister **Edward Taylor** begins writing poetry expressing his religious beliefs.

1673 French-Canadian explorer **Louis Jolliet** and French missionary **Jacques Marquette** discover the Mississippi River.

1674 New Amsterdam housewife **Maria van Cortlandt van Rensselaer** takes over management of Rensselaerswyck, a large plantation.

1675 Wampanoag chief **Metacom (King Philip)** starts King Philip's War.

1676 Virginia political dissident **Nathaniel Bacon** leads a rebellion against the Franchise Act, which restricts voting rights to a few wealthy landowners.

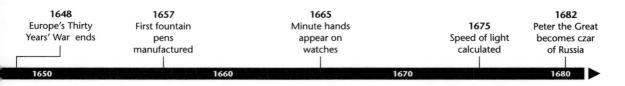

1648 Europe's Thirty Years' War ends	**1657** First fountain pens manufactured	**1665** Minute hands appear on watches	**1675** Speed of light calculated	**1682** Peter the Great becomes czar of Russia
1650	1660	1670	1680	

1676	Connecticut colonist **Mary White Rowlandson** and her children are taken captive by the Wampanoag tribe.
1679	Mohawk holy woman **Catherine (Kateri) Tekakwitha** founds a convent for Native American women.
1680	Pueblo revolutionary leader **Popé** drives the Spanish out of New Mexico.
1682	French explorer **René-Robert Cavelier de La Salle** discovers the mouth of the Mississippi River.
1682	Quaker minister **William Penn** founds Pennsylvania.
1687	Austrian Jesuit missionary **Eusebio Francisco Kino** begins his work in New Mexico.
1689	Calvinist political leader **Jacob Leisler** stages a rebellion against Catholic rule in New York.
1693	Boston clergyman and scientist **Cotton Mather** defends the Salem witch trials.
1697	British privateer **William Kidd** becomes a pirate.
1697	Massachusetts judge **Samuel Sewall** makes a public apology for his role in the Salem witch trials.
1704	Massachusetts businesswoman **Sarah Kemble Knight** writes about her trip through New England to New York City.
1720	Wealthy Virginia landowner and politician **William Byrd II** succeeds in upholding the power of the Council of Virginia.
1730	Boston portrait painter **John Smibert** gains fame as America's first artist.
1733	English social reformer **James Edward Oglethorpe** founds Georgia as a penal colony.

1692
Aesop's Fables
is published

1701
War of Spanish
Succession
begins

1714
War of Spanish
Succession ends

1721
Postal service
between
London and
New England
begins

| 1690 | 1700 | 1710 | 1720 |

1735	The not-guilty verdict in the trial of newspaper publisher **John Peter Zenger** establishes freedom of the press in America.
1739	Evangelical preacher **George Whitefield** sparks the Great Awakening, a series of religious revivals, in the American colonies.
1741	New England minister **Jonathan Edwards** delivers his famous sermon, *Sinners in the Hands of an Angry God* for the first time.
1742	Pennsylvania entrepreneur and Indian agent **George Croghan** establishes fur trade on the Ohio frontier.
1743	Scientist and inventor **Benjamin Franklin** begins his revolutionary experiments with electricity.
1743	Quaker minister **John Woolman** starts the first organized abolitionist movement.
1744	Carolina plantation manager **Eliza Lucas Pinckney** perfects the cultivation of indigo, a type of dye.
1748	German minister **Henry Melchior Mühlenberg** unites Lutheran churches in America.
1756	Eleven-year-old African prince **Olaudah Equiano** is kidnapped and sold into slavery.
1757	Botanist **Jane Colden** compiles a catalogue of native plants in the New York region.
1759	Mohegan preacher **Samson Occom** is ordained as a Christian minister.
1763	Failed rebellion staged by Ottawa war chief **Pontiac** marks the beginning of the end of the Native American way of life.

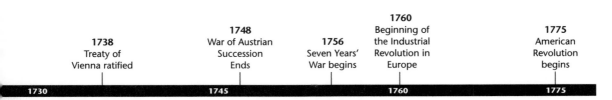

1738
Treaty of
Vienna ratified

1748
War of Austrian
Succession
Ends

1756
Seven Years'
War begins

1760
Beginning of
the Industrial
Revolution in
Europe

1775
American
Revolution
begins

| 1730 | 1745 | 1760 | 1775 |

Words to Know

A

Abolitionist: A person who takes measures to end slavery.

Absolute authority: Governing free from restraint.

American Revolution: 1775-83; a conflict in which American colonists gained independence from British rule.

Anarchist: One who rebels against any authority.

Antimonianism: The belief that faith alone is sufficient for salvation from sin. The view was considered heresy because it was contrary to the Puritan teaching that salvation can be gained only by doing good works.

B

Baptism: Initiation into the church in a ceremony that involves emersion in water or the sprinkling of water on the head.

Botanist: A specialist in plant life.

C

Calvinists: A religious group that places strong emphasis on the supreme power of God, the sinfulness of mankind, and the doctrine of predestination, which states that all human events are controlled by God.

Cannibalism: The eating of human flesh by another human being.

Capital offenses: Crimes that require a penalty of death.

Catechism: A summary or religious doctrine often in the form of questions and answers.

Charter: Title of land; a grant or guarantee from a sovereign power of a state or country.

Cholera: A disease marked by severe stomach problems.

The Church of England: The official religion of England; also known as the Anglican Church.

Classical school: A school devoted to the study of ancient languages and history.

Conquistador: Spanish military leader.

D

Decimated: Reduced drastically in number.

Dissenters: Those who question authority.

Dogma: Established opinion.

Dowry: The money or land brought by a bride to her husband at marriage.

E

Elegies: Pensive or reflective poems that are usually nostalgic or melancholy.

Emigrated: Moved from another country.

Excommunicated: Excluded from partaking in the rights of the church.

Exonerated: Cleared from accusation or blame.

F

Famine: An extreme scarcity of food.

Freeman: Former indentured servants who had gained their freedom; one who has the full rights of a citizen.

Friars: Members of a religious order who combine life as a monk with outside religious activity.

G

Great Awakening: A series of religious revivals that swept the American colonies near the middle of the eighteenth century.

H

Heretic: One who violates the laws of the church; one who does not conform to an accepted belief or doctrine.

Hybridization: The interbreeding of offspring of two animals or plants of different species.

Hydrography: The science of charting bodies of water.

I

Imported: To bring in from a foreign source.

Indentured servant: A person bound by signed documents to work as a laborer or household help for a specified time.

Insurrection: An act of revolt against civil authority or an established government.

L

Libel: Making a false statement that exposes another person to public dishonor.

M

Midwife: A person who assists women during childbirth.

Militia: Citizen's army.

Moravian Church: Sometimes known as United Brethren, it is a religion based on the forgiveness of sins through personal faith, strict interpretation of the Bible, and the importance of preaching the word of Jesus Christ instead of relying on church rituals.

Mutiny: A staged revolt or rebellion.

N

New World: A European term for North and South America.

Northwest Passage: The water route between the Atlantic and Pacific Oceans that the major world powers had long been seeking.

O

Ordained: Officially appointed with ministerial or priestly authority by the church.

Overseer: One who supervises workers.

P

Parliament: The supreme legislature body of government.

Patent: An official document giving a right to a piece of land.

Patron: One who gives financial support.

Pauper: One who cannot pay debts.

Pirate: A person who robs ships or plunders the land from the sea.

Plunderer: A person who steals by force.

Portage: To carry boats overland.

Privateer: A sailor on a privately owned ship who is authorized by a government to attack and capture enemy vessels.

Puritans: A religious group that believed in strict moral and spiritual codes.

Q

Quakers: Members of the Religious Society of Friends, which believes that the individual can receive divine truth from the Holy Spirit through his or her own "inner light" without the guidance of a minister or priest.

R

Roman Catholic Church: A Christian faith based in Rome, Italy, and headed by a pope who is considered unable of making a mistake and who oversees bishops, priests, and other clergy.

Royalists: Supporters of the king and queen.

S

Scripture: Passages from the Bible.

Scurvy: A disease caused by lack of vitamin C in the diet.

Sedition: Resistance against lawful authority.

Self-purification: Freeing oneself as an individual from sin.

Slave: A worker owned by and forced to work for someone else.

Smallpox: A highly contagious, often fatal, skin disease.

Speciman: An individual item typical of a whole.

Synod: An advisory council.

T

Tenent: A principle or doctrine.

Tenure: Term of holding a position or office.

Theologian: A specialist in the study of religion.

Topography: Configuration of a surface including the position of its natural and man-made features.

Tyrant: A ruler who brutally exercises absolute power.

V

Viceroy: One who rules in the name of the king.

W

Wampum: Beads used by Native Americans as money, ceremonial pledges, and ornaments.

Nathaniel Bacon

January 2, 1647
London, England
October, 1676
Jamestown, Virginia

Colonial leader and landowner

Nathaniel Bacon was a political leader and landowner in seventeenth-century Virginia who rose to prominence at a time when the colony was in turmoil. Wide divisions in social classes had produced a sense of unrest, especially among frontier farmers, who had little protection from Native Americans. The situation was brought to a crisis when the British governor, **William Berkeley** (see entry), adopted the Franchise Act of 1670. The law created an elite government by restricting the voting rights to a chosen few. Bacon became a popular leader when he supported farmers who felt left out of the governing process and needed protection from Native Americans who raided their farms. Bacon's Rebellion of 1676 began after Bacon raised a militia (citizens' army) and stormed the steps of the assembly building in Jamestown, Virginia. Throughout the uprising Bacon enjoyed the popular support of the people as he attempted to force Berkeley from office. Historians have debated Bacon's impact on colonial history, many linking his rebellion to the beginning of slavery in America.

"Gentlemen of your quality come very rarely into this country."

William Berkeley's comment to Nathaniel Bacon.

Portrait: Nathaniel Bacon.
Reproduced by permission of Archive Photos, Inc.

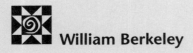

William Berkeley

William Berkeley was a controversial British colonial governor of Virginia. In 1642 he arrived in the colony to serve his first term. During his tenure (term of holding a position or office) he extended exploration of the New World (a European term for North America and South America), expanded agriculture, and defeated Native Americans and their Dutch allies. He also punished dissenters (those who question existing authority) in Virginia. In 1652 Berkeley was ousted by a group of Puritans from England. The former governor retreated to his Virginia plantation until he was reappointed by British monarchs King William III and Queen Mary II in 1660. Ten years later he established the Franchise Act, which restricted voting rights in the colony to wealthy landowners and businessmen. The Franchise Act, as well as his refusal to protect frontiersmen from Native Americans, led to an uprising known as Bacon's Rebellion of 1676, in which colonial rebel Nathaniel Bacon raised a militia against Berkeley.

Emigrates to the colony of Virginia

Nathaniel Bacon was born on January 2, 1647. According to some sources, his place of birth was London, England. His father was Thomas Bacon of Friston Hall, Suffolk, and his cousin was Lord Chancellor Francis Bacon. As a young man, Bacon attended Cambridge University and Gray's Inn, a school of law. After graduating he traveled throughout Europe. In 1673 he married Elizabeth Duke, daughter of Edward Duke. They emigrated (moved from another country) to the Virginia colony and settled at Curl's Neck in Henrico County, on the James River near the border of Native American territory. Because of Bacon's political abilities and social connections, he quickly gained influence in the colony. His uncle was a member of the government council, which led to the younger Bacon being appointed to a seat on the council. Being of a rebellious nature, Bacon set out to change the system as soon as he took office. He aligned himself with the common people and strove to solve their problems.

Roots of rebellion

Colonial America was a land in turmoil during the late seventeenth century. Most of the trouble was centered in Virginia, England's most treasured colony. This unrest led directly to Bacon's Rebellion, which occurred in 1676. The roots of the insurrection (an act of revolt against civil authority or an established government) can be traced back sixteen years, to 1660, when William Berkeley was reappointed governor of Virginia. At first Berkeley was popular with the people, but this support began to fade. Historians point out that a major factor in his decline was his willingness to give power in Virginia to English merchants at the expense of other citizens. Evidence for this view was the Franchise Act of 1670, a law that gave voting rights only to landowners and people who owned houses. This enabled him to surround himself with a small elite government, the Green Spring faction, which he named for his Green Spring plantation. Meanwhile, the remainder of the population were indentured servants (people bound by signed documents to work as laborers or household help for a specified time) who could not afford land and thus could not obtain the right to vote. Soon there was widespread unrest in Virginia.

Colonists seek revenge

Despite these problems, the colony began to grow. As a consequence of expansion, the borders of the settlement eventually reached Native American territory. The Virginia colonizers generally did not get along with the native peoples, whom they often accused of stealing from their farms. This tension between colonists and Native Americans led to violence. One of the first serious incidents occurred in 1675, when members of the Doeg tribe killed an overseer (one who supervises workers) on a plantation. The Virginia government responded by forming a militia led by Colonel George Mason and Captain John Brent. When the militia attacked two Native American cabins, they did not realize that members of the Susquehannock tribe were inside instead of Doegs. After killing fourteen Susquehannocks, the militia continued their advance. Five Susquehannock chiefs immediately protested that the colonists had been killed by a Seneca war party, not by Susquehannocks. The Virginians refused to believe them, claiming Susquehannocks had recently been seen in the area, wearing the clothes of the white victims. The Virginians then executed the chiefs.

When the Susquehannocks began to retaliate, the fighting escalated. At this point Berkeley tried to end the conflict by declining to launch another attack. Many Virginians protested, accusing him of trying to protect the fur trade with Native Americans. They contended that the fur trade was important to Berkeley because it made a lot of money for the economy and ensured his support among local, wealthy merchants. This conflict only served to distance Berkeley even

Bacon issues proclamation

During his famous rebellion, colonial leader Nathaniel Bacon stormed the steps of the assembly building in Jamestown, Virginia, to demand action for his followers. On July 30, 1676, he issued a declaration "In the Name of the People of Virginia." His goal was to rally popular support by undermining the British governor of the colony, William Berkeley. Bacon had initially come into power after raising a militia of frontier farmers who protested Berkeley's reluctance to retaliate against Native American border raids. In a manifesto known as "Bacon's Laws," Bacon attacked Berkeley for raising unfair taxes "for the advancement of private favorites and other sinister ends." He also accused Berkeley of selling out Virginia to the fur trade when he "wronged his Majesty's prerogative and interest by assuming monopoly [exclusive control] of the beaver trade." Bacon claimed that Berkeley even allowed Native Americans to murder Virginians by not "appointing any due or proper means of satisfaction for their many invasions, robberies, and murders committed upon us."

While Bacon received widespread support, many Virginians continued to align themselves with Berkeley. In 1676 the citizens of Gloucester County sent a letter to Berkeley pledging their continued support of his leadership. They praised the governor "for securing our neighbors [and] the frontiers of this country from the incursions of the barbarous Indians." Even though Bacon had also raised a militia to fight Native Americans, these citizens cited his lawlessness in requesting more resources from the county with orders "grounded, as he pretends, upon a commission from your Honor to be general of all the forces in Virginia against the Indians." They were mostly disturbed by the behavior of Bacon and his men who "did in many places behave themselves very rudely both in words and actions."

more from the new Virginia colonizers, especially the citizens of Charles and Henrico counties. Frontiersmen in these outlying areas wanted to continue fighting to protect their property. Since they could get no leadership from Berkeley, they turned instead to Bacon. He rallied the frontiersmen to form their own militia, with reinforcements from the Ocaneechee tribe. The newly formed militia immediately tracked down a group of Susquehannocks and defeated them. Berkeley was furious with Bacon and declared him a traitor.

Berkeley tries to regain power

After witnessing Bacon's rise to power, Berkeley became aware of the decline in his own popularity. Therefore, in May 1676 he ordered new elections and issued a declaration. He defended himself as governor of Virginia and suggested several measures through which he hoped to redeem himself. The legislative assembly met in Jamestown on June 5 to act on Berkeley's proposals. Of all the actions he wanted to take, three are considered the most important. First, he planned to pardon Bacon and give him a commission to raise a militia against Native Americans. Second, Berkeley wanted to draft a measure that permitted Virginians to trade only with "friendly Indians." Third, he planned to abolish the Franchise Act of 1670, thus restoring the vote to all freemen (former indentured servants who had gained their freedom), not just landowners.

Bacon leads rebellion

The Virginia legislators approved all three of these proposals. Nevertheless, Bacon rejected the plan because they planned to draw militia members from the entire colony, whereas Bacon wanted to use men from the border territories because he thought they would be more effective and more likely to cooperate than men from other parts of the colony. Also, he demanded to begin immediately instead of waiting for three months until taxes had been raised for the militia. On June 23, 1676, he led 400 armed men up the steps of the Jamestown assembly hall. Bacon's Rebellion had begun. A confrontation ensued and Bacon threatened violence. After forcing the assembly to exempt (free or release from liability) him and his men from prosecution for causing a disturbance, Bacon eventually left with his followers. A humiliated Berkeley declared Bacon a traitor once again, then called up the colonial militia. When Bacon and his men returned on July 30, Berkeley fled to the eastern coast. This time Bacon carried with him a manifesto (statement) titled "In the Name of the People of Virginia," which accused Berkeley of committing numerous injustices. With Berkeley absent, Bacon now had control of Jamestown. When he led his men out into the country and attacked the Pawmunkey tribe, Berkeley returned. On September 18 Bacon launched a final assault on Jamestown, burning

the settlement to the ground. By now lawlessness reigned and
Berkeley escaped again as looters (robbers) ransacked his plantation at Green Spring.

Bacon's Rebellion might have lasted much longer if
Bacon himself had not become ill and died the following October. After his death, the insurrection was put down by Berkeley, who executed twenty-three of Bacon's men—in spite of a

royal order pardoning all participants except Bacon. Berkeley finally gave up his position as governor to Colonel Herbert Jeffreys, who appointed a commission to investigate the uprising. The commission members mostly blamed Bacon and his ability to influence the leaderless frontiersmen.

Significance of Bacon's Rebellion?

Historians have long debated the impact of Bacon's Rebellion on colonial American life. In the nineteenth century many thought the insurrection was a bid for American independence from England, and that Bacon was a heroic predecessor to George Washington, a revered leader in the American Revolution (1775–83; a conflict in which American colonists gained independence from British rule). Other scholars pointed out, however, that Bacon had no clear philosophy of liberation and he was not fighting the English. They also suggested that the rebellion was mainly a result of a personal grudge between Bacon and Berkeley. Therefore, because Bacon put his own interests ahead of those of the colony, he is less of a hero. Some historians have even linked Bacon's Rebellion to the beginning of slavery in America. They point out that after the insurrection, colonists decided that African slaves were easier to control than indentured servants.

For further reference

Bacon's Rebellion. http://www.infoplease.com/ce5/CE00404.5.html Available July 13, 1999.

Harrah, Madge. *My Brother, My Enemy.* New York: Simon & Schuster Books for Young Readers, 1997. (Fiction)

Middleton, Richard. *Colonial America: A History, 1585–1776,* second edition. Malden, Mass: Blackwell, 1996, pp. 149–54.

Nathaniel Bacon, Manifesto. http://planetx.bloom.edu/_aholton/121readings_html/bacon Available July 13, 1999.

Webb, Stephen Saunders. *1676: The End of American Independence.* New York: Knopf, 1984.

John Bartram

March 23, 1699
Marple, Delaware County, Pennsylvania
September 22, 1777
Kingsessing, Pennsylvania

Botanist and gardener

John Bartram, an eighteenth-century botanist (a specialist in plant life), was well known in colonial America and Europe. He grew up in Pennsylvania, where he was inspired by the beautiful countryside to study nature. As a young man, Bartram ventured to the nearby city of Philadelphia, one of the scientific centers of colonial America, where he met important scientific figures of the time, including James Logan. He introduced Bartram to the study of botany and, through Logan, Bartram became acquainted with the work of the great Swedish botanist Carolus Linnaeus. Bartram is best known for the five-acre botanical garden, called "the Garden," that he began planting at Kingsessing, Pennsylvania, in 1728. While conducting a correspondence with English botanist Peter Collinson, Bartram imported (to bring from a foreign external source) rare and exotic plant specimens. (A specimen is an individual item typical of a whole.) Because of its extensive variety of plant species, the Garden was the pride of the colonial American scientific community. While conducting expeditions throughout the countryside of the eastern colonies, Bartram commented not only on the plant life, but on the cultural aspects of the colonies as well. These proved to be an insightful and influential study of early America.

Inspired by local countryside

John Bartram was born on March 23, 1699, in Marple, which is located near Darby in Delaware County, Pennsylvania. His father was William Bartram, and his mother was Elizabeth Hunt. Bartram's grandfather, John Bartram, had settled near Darby after leaving England in 1682. When Bartram was born several years later in 1699, his extended family had already been Quakers for three generations. (The Quakers, members of the Religious Society of Friends, believe that the individual can receive divine truth from the Holy Spirit through his or her own "inner light" without the guidance of a minister or priest.) Bartram himself remained a Quaker all his life. However, as he grew older and learned more about science and nature, he found it increasingly difficult to remain an orthodox Quaker (one who conforms to established doctrine).

Bartram first became interested in nature as a young man. He was particularly intrigued by the beautiful Pennsylvania countryside south of Philadelphia. As he was growing up, Bartram increasingly spent his time outdoors. In order to acquire more information about his newfound fascination, Bartram traveled to Philadelphia, where he could find the appropriate books on plants. It was there that he met James Logan, an influential Philadelphia scientific scholar and patron (one who gives financial support). Logan introduced Bartram to Latin, which was the language of scientific correspondence. Logan also loaned books to Bartram, helped him master the microscope, and turned the young man's attention to the work of the great Swedish botanist Carolus Linnaeus. Bartram eventually carried on a fruitful correspondence with Linnaeus.

Bartram was married twice during his lifetime. In 1723 he wed Mary Morris, with whom he had two sons. After her death, Bartram married Ann Mendenhall in 1729. With

Swedish botanist Carolus Linnaeus's work was a great influence on Bartram.
Reproduced by permission of the Library of Congress.

Mendenhall, Bartram had five sons and four daughters. One of his sons from his second marriage was named William who, like his father, became a great botanist.

Starts botanical garden

Even though Bartram studied important books about plants early in his career, he preferred to grow plants rather than read about them. This enthusiasm for nature led Bartram to gather and distribute plants. He also became an accomplished gardener. In 1728 Bartram began his great five-acre Garden on land he purchased in Kingsessing, Pennsylvania, three miles from Philadelphia on the banks of the Schuylkill River. After laying out the Garden, he conducted what might have been the first experiments in hybridization (interbreeding of offspring of two animals or plants of different breeds) in America.

One of Bartram's activities as a gardener was the trading of plants with other botanists throughout the world. Mainly, he received requests for plant and animal specimens from European scientists. In about 1733 Bartram began a correspondence with the English botanist Peter Collinson. Bartram and Collinson were both Quakers, and although they became lifelong friends, they never met. Their letter exchange greatly benefitted both men. Bartram fulfilled Collinson's endless requests for specimens of butterflies and such trees as sasparilla, cypress, white cedar, laurel, and locust. In return Collinson sent seeds from plants found in England and Europe that Bartram planted in the Garden.

Bartram was so accommodating that Collinson found other patrons for his activities. Bartram conducted correspondences with Mark Catesby, Hans Sloane, John Fothergill, J. F. Gronovius, and other leading European scientists. Gaining fame in Europe, he even corresponded with Linnaeus, who believed that Bartram was the greatest botanist in the world at the time. Bartram also corresponded with American colleagues of Linnaeus, including Alexander Garden, Cadwallader Colden (see box in **Jane Colden** entry), John Mitchell, and John Clayton. As a result of these contacts and the constant exchange of plants between America and Europe, Bartram's Garden became varied and exotic. In fact, it was the talk of the entire colonial American scientific community. Even scientist and statesman **Benjamin Franklin** (see entry) and future American president George Washington would stop in the Garden to view the beautiful plants and have philosophical conversations. Despite Bartram's worldwide reputation, however, he continued to be a humble farmer.

Travels throughout colonial America

In addition to being an active gardener, Bartram traveled thousands of miles throughout America collecting specimens of plant life. There were few regions that Bartram did not visit. In 1738 he journeyed 1,100 miles through Maryland and Virginia and crossed the Blue Ridge Mountains. Four years later, he traveled up the Hudson River to the Catskill Mountains, journeyed along the Schuylkill and Susquehanna Rivers in Pennsylvania, and crossed the Allegheny Mountains to upstate New York and Lake Ontario. Along the way he made notes on the topography (configuration of a surface including the position of its natural and man-made features) and described Native American customs. Bartram's account of his journeys was published in London as *Observations on the Inhabitants, Climate, Soil, Rivers, Productions, Animals, and Other Matters Worthy of Notice* (1751). Beginning in 1754 Bartram took his son William, the future botanist, along with him on his travels. In 1761, during a trip to Pittsburgh, Pennsylvania—which was then a fort on the western frontier—Bartram encountered a group of Native Americans. One of them reportedly snatched his hat and began eating it. A distressed Bartram interpreted this act as a threat of cannibalism (the eating human flesh by a human being).

In 1765, through the help of Collinson, Bartram became the royal botanist to King George III of England. This position involved the study and description of plant life in North America, and he immediately set off for Charleston (in present-day South Carolina) to observe plant life in the South. Bartram then traveled by land through Georgia to Saint Augustine, Florida. After obtaining a canoe, he explored the San Juan (St. John's) River and prepared a detailed map of the waterway. During this expedition Bartram also discovered the royal palm tree. This was considered an important finding because the royal palm is rare and can be found only in the southernmost part of Florida and Cuba.

Remembered as influential American

After taking his numerous journeys, Bartram became disappointed that most Americans were not more interested in nature or science. He also disagreed with colonial Americans on the issue of slavery. A strong abolitionist (a person who takes measures to end slavery), he freed his own slaves even though it was unpopular to do so at the time. They remained in his household as paid servants and regularly took meals with the Bartram family and guests. Bartram was an enthusiastic scientist throughout his life, collecting shells, birds, insects, fish, and turtles. Acquiring an interest in geology (study of the Earth), he proposed the creation of a map of the rocks underlying the vast American landscape. This job was eventually performed by the United States Geological Survey. Bartram also suggested a massive voyage to survey the American West. Historians speculate that this idea was later passed on by Franklin to President Thomas Jefferson and may have led to the famous expedition headed by Meriwether Lewis and William Clark in search of an overland route to the Pacific Ocean (1803–06). Meanwhile, the Garden at Kingsessing remained one of the greatest in the world. Over the years, it has been studied by many prominent naturalists. The first memorial to an American botanist, the Garden later became part of the Philadelphia park system.

For further reference

Berkeley, Edmund, and Dorothy Smith Berkeley. *The Life and Travels of John Bartram from Lake Ontario to the River St. John.* Tallahassee: University Presses of Florida, 1982.

Herbst, Josephine. *New Green World.* New York: Hastings House, 1954.

Historic Bartram's Garden. http://www.libertynet.org/bartram/story/index .html Available July 13, 1999.

Slaughter, Thomas P. *The Natures of John and William Bartram.* New York: Vintage Books, 1997.

William Bradford

1590
Austerfield, Yorkshire, England
May 9, 1657
Plymouth Colony

Governor and historian

Willliam Bradford was the leader of a religious group called the Pilgrims, who embarked on the famous voyage to the New World (the European term for North America and South America) on board the ship *Mayflower*. In 1620, after landing on the northeast coast of present-day Massachusetts, the Pilgrims established Plymouth Colony. When the first elected governor, John Carver, died, Bradford took his place. As governor, Bradford grappled with a terrible famine (an extreme scarcity of food) and forged relations with local Native Americans. Bradford's time in office is considered an example of effective early American politics. Although he practiced absolute authority, he was not a tyrant (a ruler who exercises absolute power brutally). In addition to being the governor of Plymouth, Bradford was also an important religious leader and its principal historian. He wrote *Of Plymouth Plantation* (1630), which remains a valuable source of information about life in colonial America.

Leaves England with Nonconformists

William Bradford was born in 1590 at Austerfield, Yorkshire, in England. His father was William Bradford, a

"And here is to be noted a special providence of God, and a great mercy to this poor people, that here they got seed to plant them corn the next year, or else they might have starved. . . . "

William Bradford.

Portrait: William Bradford.
Reproduced by permission of the Bettmann Archive.

13

wealthy landowner. His mother, Alice, was the daughter of John Hanson, a village shopkeeper. He was their third child and only son. When his father died on July 15, 1591, Bradford inherited an ample fortune. After his mother died a few years later, he was left in the care of his grandfather and uncles.

Bradford's uncles taught him how to farm, and he probably planned to take over his father's estate one day. When he was twelve years old, however, he became deeply involved in religion. Against the wishes of his family he joined a religious group that called themselves the Nonconformists—later known as Puritans—because they refused to conform to the laws of the Church of England (the official religion of England, also known as the Anglican Church). Their meetings, which were conducted by the Reverend Richard Clyfton, took place in the house of a local postmaster, William Brewster, in Scrooby, Nottinghamshire. At that time England was at the height of the Protestant Reformation, a religious revolution within the Roman Catholic Church that began sweeping across Western Europe in the previous century. (The Protestant Reformation was started by German theologian Martin Luther, who accused Catholic leaders of corruption and misuse of power.) By the early 1600s the spirit of reform had also influenced Protestant groups who were intent on self-purification (freeing themselves as individuals from sin). The Nonconformists believed the Church of England had become far too corrupt to benefit from reforms. They also feared that the king, Charles I, was sympathetic to Catholics. Because of these beliefs, the Nonconformists decided to separate from the Church of England. Since this was considered an act of treason, the Nonconformists were forced to leave England or be punished by imprisonment or even death. In 1608 Bradford joined their migration to Amsterdam, Holland. A year later the Nonconformists settled in Leiden, the Netherlands, where they were allowed to practice their religion freely. By 1611 Bradford was old enough to convert his inheritance into cash. Afterwards, he bought a loom (a frame or machine used to weave cloth) and went into the textile (fabric or cloth) trade. In 1613 Bradford married Dorothy Day and settled in Leiden.

Sails on *Mayflower*

The Nonconformists remained in Leiden for only a short time. Many younger members, including Bradford,

found that making a living was very difficult, and they searched for an area where they could practice their religion and also keep their English traditions and language, even if it meant living under English rule. They petitioned the Virginia Company (a private organization that promoted colonization of the Virginia territory) of London, England, and were granted a patent (an official document giving a right or privilege) for land in the Virginia territory. On September 5, 1620, the group, which Bradford called "Pilgrims," set sail on the *Mayflower* for the New World.

Along the way the *Mayflower* encountered stormy weather, and the Pilgrims never arrived in Virginia. Instead they anchored the ship in Cape Cod harbor (off the coast of present-day Massachusetts), a spot that was far north of their original destination. Since that land had not been legally granted to them, Bradford and the Pilgrims drafted and signed the Mayflower Compact in November 1620, a document that claimed ownership of the area. Because the Pilgrims accounted

The landing of the Pilgrims at Plymouth, Massachusetts, in 1620. *Reproduced by permission of Archive Photos, Inc.*

for only forty percent of the people aboard the ship, the agreement also set out to guarantee security against dissension (discord or quarreling) with the rest of the passengers. These settlers, men such as Miles Standish, were outsiders whom the Pilgrims called "strangers." The agreement also provided for a government as well as a new religious society. Although the Mayflower Compact is considered the first democracy established by Europeans in North America there is little proof to support this claim.

Plymouth Colony founded

While the *Mayflower* was anchored in Cape Cod harbor in November 1620, Bradford joined an expedition led by Standish. Leaving the *Mayflower* in a small boat, they entered the harbor, which they called Plymouth harbor, and landed near a rock that is now known as Plymouth Rock. The Pilgrims settled their new colony in December and elected Carver as their first governor. After Carver died in April 1621, Bradford was immediately chosen to take his place. He would be reelected thirty times between 1621 and 1656. During this period, Bradford repeatedly tried to quit the governorship, but he was such an effective and beloved leader that colonists always wanted him to remain in office. Tragically, Bradford's wife drowned in Cape Cod harbor on December 7, 1620. Three years later he was remarried, to a woman named Alice Carpenter Southworth.

Forges relations with Native Americans

Conditions in Plymouth were harsh, and Bradford did all he could as governor to save the colony from disaster. The Pilgrims were devastated by sickness—over half of the population perished—and only a few men were left to do the farming for the colony. Their first winter, in 1620–21, was especially bleak. In the spring the local Wampanoag tribe, led by Chief **Massasoit** (see entry), taught the Pilgrims how to plant crops such as barley, peas, and corn. Massasoit asked Squanto, another prominent Wampanoag who spoke the English language, to head the effort to help the colonists. (As a teenager Squanto was kidnapped and sold into slavery in Spain, then eventually made his way to England, where he spent a few years.) Squanto is remembered today as the person who saved the Pilgrims from starvation, and he is closely associated with

Bradford writes history of Plymouth

As the principal historian of the Plymouth Colony, William Bradford began writing *Of Plymouth Plantation* in 1630. He gave a detailed account of the Pilgrims' journey to Plymouth and the subsequent hardships they faced in the New World. It is said that Bradford wrote the history because Massachusetts Bay colonist **John Winthrop** (see entry) began writing a similar document in 1630 about the Puritan migration. Bradford described the early optimism and faith of the Pilgrims and their eventual corruption by adverse forces. In Book I he compared the Pilgrims to the Israelites of the Old Testament (the first part of the Bible), who traveled out of captivity to the Promised Land. Yet the Pilgrims' battle against evil did not end when they reached the New World. In the opening part of his work, Bradford mentions the "wars and oppositions" that "Satan hath raised, maintained and continued against the saints" in the Plymouth Colony.

In 1646 Bradford started Book II, which is even less optimistic than Book I.

By now the Pilgrims had experienced famine and the treachery of "merchant adventurers," businessmen who took advantage of the colonists. They also had conflicts with Native Americans. The Pequot War of 1637 became a major turning point: New England colonists formed an alliance with the Narragansett tribe and attacked a Pequot fort, killing four hundred Pequots in their sleep. Over time, Bradford came to realize that evil comes from people themselves and not simply through the magical power of Satan. He wrote that the Pilgrims had arrived in the New World "knit together as a body in a most strict and sacred bond and covenant of the Lord." He later added, "But (alas) that subtle serpent hath slyly wound in himself under fair pretenses of necessity and the like, to untwist these sacred bonds and ties." Over time Plymouth became less focused on religion and eventually merged with the more prosperous Massachusetts Bay Colony.

the first Thanksgiving. After a bountiful harvest in the fall, the Pilgrims and Wampanoags celebrated the "first Thanksgiving." Another problem for the Pilgrims was that they had no resources for businesses such as fur trading, which was thriving in other colonies, because they knew little about commerce. Pilgrim leaders paid attention to immediate needs rather than long-term plans. Yet they were not completely unskilled in politics and business, having gained experience in

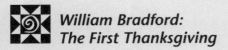

William Bradford: The First Thanksgiving

During their first winter in the Plymouth Colony (1620–21), the Pilgrims were devastated by sickness—over half of the population perished—and only a few men were left to do the farming for the colony. In the spring the local Wampanoag tribe, led by Chief Massasoit, taught the Pilgrims how to plant crops such as barley, peas, and corn. After a bountiful harvest in the fall, the Pilgrims and Wampanoags celebrated the "first Thanksgiving." This event is portrayed in *William Bradford: The First Thanksgiving* (1992), a thirty-minute animated film originally broadcast on the Family Entertainment television network. The film is available on videocassette.

self-government through their handling of church affairs. Bradford regarded Plymouth as the site of the New World church for Nonconformists who remained in Europe. Therefore, despite extreme food shortages, he invited more Nonconformists to move to Plymouth from Leiden.

As the colony grew, Bradford recognized the need to befriend more local Native Americans. Although Bradford and the Pilgrims had formed an alliance with Massasoit, who was highly regarded by area tribes, the Pilgrims were threatened by the Narragansett tribe. Further conflict came when Massasoit warned that a group of natives was planning to attack the colonists. On the advice of Massasoit, the troublemakers were rounded up and killed. Bradford never wanted a confrontation with Native Americans, since by keeping good relations with them he was able to alleviate the famine. He eventually achieved peaceful trading relationships with the natives and increased the food supply in Plymouth. Nevertheless this harmony was disturbed when the colonists found themselves in the middle of battles between the Narragansetts and the Mohegans. Tensions continued to mount, and in the Pequot War (1637) the New England colonies united with the Narragansetts to attack a Pequot fort at Mystic, Connecticut. As a result, four hundred Pequots were killed in their sleep.

Deals with "merchant adventurers"

The Native Americans were not the only group that caused problems for the upright Pilgrims at Plymouth. They also had to contend with the "strangers," or those who were not Pilgrims. Many of these men came over on the *Mayflower* as servants, and others were already in North America. Known also as "merchant adventurers," they represented businessmen in London. Men such as Standish, John Alden, and Richard

Warren were useful to Bradford. However, many "merchant adventurers," who had names like "Oldham the mad trader" and "Lyford the lewd parson," were criminals and tried to cheat the colonists. Bradford dealt with these men the best he could, usually forgiving their crimes.

In 1627, Bradford made a business deal that benefitted the entire colony. His plan called for the Pilgrims to buy out the merchant adventurers and divide their property evenly among the colonists. As a result, the outcast merchants became part of the Pilgrim society and Bradford labeled them "Old Comers." In order to buy them out, Bradford joined seven Pilgrims and four merchants from London in taking on the debt. These twelve men, known as the "Undertakers," began engaging in fishing and trading businesses in order to raise money. However, they had little success with these ventures. In 1631 they still owed money after some of the "Undertakers" resigned. Bradford, Standish, and Alden all had to sell land to pay off the rest of the debt.

Given absolute authority

During his first few years in office, Bradford frequently practiced absolute authority (governing free from restraint). Although historians have labeled the Plymouth Colony a democracy, there is little proof to support this claim. The people who signed the Mayflower Compact may have exercised power as a group, but they gave all authority to the governor. When Bradford became governor in 1621, he served as principal judge and treasurer until 1637. He oversaw trade and agriculture, managed profits, and assigned plots of land to settlers. Since he held executive and legislative authority, only he could decide when freemen (former indentured servants who had earned their freedom) were allowed to take part in government. Bradford was also allowed to make decisions without the advice of other government authorities and businessmen.

Throughout his career, Bradford never showed any desire for power and gain. In 1630, the "Warwick Patent" was granted to him from the Council for New England. This document made Bradford, and whoever else he chose, proprietors (owners) of Plymouth. He immediately shared his rights with the "Old Comers." In 1636 Bradford joined a committee that drafted laws defining the duties of the governor, his assistant, and the general court. They also defined seven capital offenses (crimes that require the death penalty). In 1639 the grand jury of Plymouth protested the power possessed by the "Old Comers." It was finally decided by the court that Bradford should give up the "Warwick Patent" to freemen. This is the only known challenge of Bradford's authority as governor.

Writes history

In addition to being governor of Plymouth, Bradford was also considered its principal historian. He began writing *Of Plymouth Plantation,* Book I, in 1630 (the work was published in 1856). In this segment he portrays the Pilgrims as being optimistic about their prospects in the New World, which they considered the "Promised Land." Bradford started Book II in 1646 after many years of hardship in Plymouth. The optimism of Book I is dampened by the realization that corrupt men, not an invisible evil force like Satan, were responsible for the downfall of the colony. Bradford maintained his faith in the goodness of God, however, and continued as governor of Plymouth until the end of his life. He tried to forge relations with the wealthy and powerful Massachusetts Bay Colony, but met resistance from Massachusetts Bay residents. He also welcomed the "Great Migration" of 20,000 Puritans (1628–42) to New England. Bradford died on May 9, 1657, in Plymouth Colony. His efforts at colonial union were fulfilled in 1692 when the Plymouth Colony finally merged with the Massachusetts Bay Colony.

For further reference

Elliott, Emory, and others, eds. *American Literature: A Prentice Hall Anthology.* Englewood Cliffs, New Jersey, 1991, pp. 66–67.

Hays, Wilma Pitchford. *Rebel Pilgrim: A Biography of Governor William Bradford.* Philadelphia: Westminster Press, 1969.

Johnson, Allen, and others, eds. *Dictionary of American Biography.* New York: Scribner, pp. 559–63.

Stephen, Leslie, and Sidney Lee, eds. *The Dictionary of National Biography.* London, England: Oxford University Press, 1917, pp. 1069–73.

"William Bradford" in *The Puritans: American Literature Colonial Period (1608-1700).* http://falcon.jmu.edu/-ramseyil/amicol.htm Available July 13, 1999.

William Bradford: The First Thanksgiving. Family Entertainment Network, 1992. Videocassette recording.

Anne Bradstreet

**1612
Northampton, England
September 16, 1672
North Andover, Massachusetts**

Colonial American poet

Anne Bradstreet is considered one of America's most important colonial poets. Born in England, she was one of many Puritans (a religious group who believed in strict moral and spiritual codes) who emigrated to North America in 1630. Despite having to endure a difficult life in the New World (a European term for North America and South America), Bradstreet still managed to write poetry. In fact, she achieved many important firsts. Along with being the first published poet in colonial America, she was also the first American woman poet. In addition, her collection of verse, *The Tenth Muse* (1650), was the first written in America. Her poem "Contemplations" (1645) was the first poem to be inspired by the American landscape. Today, Bradstreet's work remains as a tribute to her intellect and passion and as a valuable source of information about the role of women in Puritan society.

Receives excellent education

Anne Dudley Bradstreet was born in Northampton, England, in 1612. She was the second of six children born to Thomas and Dorothy Dudley. Her father was a clerk and a

"All things within this fading world hath end,/

Adversity doth still our joys attend. . . . "

From Anne Bradstreet's poem "Before the Birth of One of Her Children."

member of the gentry (upper or ruling class). In 1619, when he became steward (one employed in a large estate to manage domestic concerns) to Theophilus Clinton, Earl of Lincoln, he moved his family to the earl's estate in Sempringham. At the time the estate was one of the centers of Puritan learning and activism. Leading Puritan ministers often preached in the earl's chapel, and many of the Puritan gentry and nobility met there to have discussions. As a result, the Dudley family was exposed to some of the finest preaching and intellectual debate in England.

Bradstreet received an excellent education at the earl's estate. She had private tutors, and she read many books from the earl's extensive library. The ambitious young pupil studied theology, philosophy, and literature, and she learned to appreciate music and art. At nine years old, she met her future husband, Simon Bradstreet, who was the son of a Puritan minister and a graduate of Cambridge University. He had come to Sempringham to be an assistant to Thomas Dudley. The couple were married in 1628, when Anne was only sixteen.

Travels to the New World

The newlyweds moved to the estate of the dowager (a widow holding property or a title from her deceased husband) countess of Warwick, where Simon had become steward. They did not remain there for long, however, because the religious situation in England had begun to worsen for Puritans. In 1625 King Charles I inherited the throne from his father, James I. Charles I favored William Laud, a bishop in the Church of England (also known as the Anglican Church, the official national religion), who used his influence to exclude Puritans from holding political office. As part of his effort to limit the role of Puritans in government, Charles I suspended parliament (the supreme legislative body) in 1629. All Puritans in England, including the Bradstreets and the Dudleys, were now forced to recognize that they were losing influence in the government and could possibly be in danger.

In response to this challenge to their power, Puritan leaders hoped to influence England to reform by establishing a Puritan settlement in America. In 1630 the Bradstreets and the Dudleys joined other Puritans, including lawyer **John**

"Before the Birth of One of her Children"

Modern readers marvel at the ability of Anne Bradstreet to find time to write poetry while taking care of eight children. However, judging from the subject matter of much of her poetry, the two experiences were similar. Bradstreet often wrote about her personal life, which sometimes included the fear of death in childbirth. An example of this is the following poem, titled "Before the Birth of One of Her Children":

All things within this fading world hath end,
Adversity doth still our joys attend;
No ties so strong, no friends so dear
   and sweet,
But with death's parting blow is sure
   to meet.
The sentence past is most irrevocable,
A common thing, yet oh, inevitable.
How soon, my Dear, death may my
   steps attend,
How soon't may be thy lot to lose thy friend,
We both are ignorant, yet love bids me
These farewell lines to recommend thee,
That when that knot's untied that made
   us one,
I may seem thine, who in effect am none.
And if I see not half my days that's due,
What nature would, God grant to yours
   and you;
The many faults that well you know I have

Let be interred in my oblivious grave;
If any worth or virtue were in me,
Let that live freshly in thy memory
And when thou feel'st no grief, as I
   no harms,
Yet love thy dead, who long lay in
   thine arms.
And when thy loss shall be repaid
   with gains
Look to my little babes, my dear remains.
And if thou love thyself, or love'st me,
These O protect from step-dame's injury.
And if chance to thine eyes shall bring
   this verse,
With some sad sighs honour my
   absent hearse;
And kiss this paper for thy love's dear sake,
Who with salt tears this last farewell
   did take.

This poem is a prime example of the hardship that Bradstreet portrays in her work. Since much of her poetry was introspective (an examination of one's own thoughts and feelings), it reveals how she felt about life in the New World—an existence so unpredictable and harsh that love was the only thing people could depend upon. Published in 1678, "Before the Birth of One of Her Children" was written sometime between 1640 and 1652.

Winthrop Jr. (see entry) and preacher **John Cotton** (see entry), and set out aboard the ship *Arbella* for North America. Along the way they formed the Massachusetts Bay Company. Bradstreet's father was elected deputy governor, and her husband became an assistant. Having begun their journey in April, they arrived at Salem harbor in June.

Settles in Massachusetts

Bradstreet was surprised by the harsh climate and rustic (very simple) surroundings she encountered when she arrived in North America. She realized immediately that it contrasted starkly with the privileged existence she had known in England. Yet, "convinced it was the way of God," she "submitted to it." After the families settled in Newtowne (now Cambridge), Massachusetts, Bradstreet joined the church in Boston. Since her husband and father held high positions in the Massachusetts Bay Company, Bradstreet led a relatively comfortable life, despite her difficult surroundings. She apparently found time to write because the earliest of her surviving poems, "Upon a Fit of Sickness," dates from 1632. Composed while Bradstreet was ill and hovering near death, this poem reflects the somber reality of the New World.

The Bradstreet family moved several times over the next two decades. During this period Bradstreet devoted herself to domestic life and gave birth to eight children. She had her first child, Simon, in 1633. Later Bradstreet described her family in a poem titled "In Reference to Her Children" (1678): "I had eight birds hatched in one nest/Four Cocks there were, and Hens the rest." In 1635 the Bradstreets moved from Newtowne to Ipswich, Massachusetts. Here, despite her demanding domestic responsibilities and the hardships of frontier life, Bradstreet began to write poetry in earnest. She also continued to grow intellectually in Ipswich, where she had contact with colonial leaders such as John Winthrop Jr., son of Massachusetts Bay governor John Winthrop, and Nathaniel Ward. In 1645 the Bradstreets moved to North Andover, Massachusetts. Finally settled, Bradstreet lived there for the rest of her life.

The Tenth Muse published

Even though it was unusual for women to follow intellectual pursuits at the time, Bradstreet's family took great pride in her work. They encouraged her to continue writing, and in 1647 her brother-in-law, John Woodbridge, brought a manuscript of thirteen of her poems to England. The book was published in 1650 without Bradstreet's knowledge. Titled *The Tenth Muse Lately Sprung Up in America,* it was the first collection of poetry written in America. Although *The Tenth Muse* is an important piece of American literature, there is very little

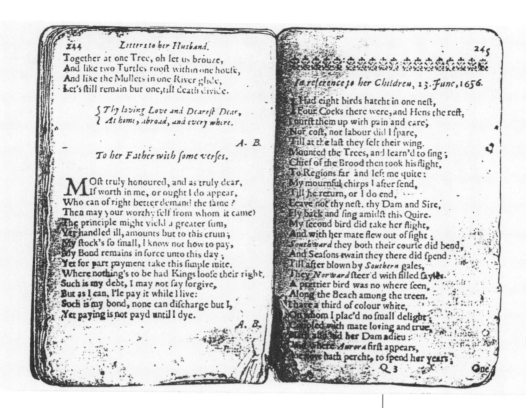

Two pages of manuscript from Anne Bradstreet's *Poems.* Reproduced by permission of The Granger Collection Ltd.

mention of the New World in the poems of the collection. In fact, the many classical allusions (references to ancient Greek and Roman literature) in the poetry harken back to the days when Bradstreet studied in the comfort of the earl's library in England. *The Tenth Muse* is not considered to be her best work, because many critics believe that she did not find her true poetic voice until later.

Among the poems in *The Tenth Muse* are elegies (pensive or reflective poems that are usually nostalgic or melancholy) and historical poetry, which reveal Bradstreet's intellectual interests. Although she read science and literature, she was mainly drawn to history—possibly because she participated in the great Puritan migration to the New World. The Puritans believed their journey was part of God's plan to banish evil from the world. She modeled much of her poetry on John Sylvester's translation of *Divine Weeks and Works* (1621) by French Calvinist poet Guillaume Du Bartas. (The Calvinists were a religious group that placed strong emphasis on the supreme power of God, the sinfulness of mankind, and the doctrine of predestination, which states that all human events are controlled by God.) Another major influence was *History of the World* (1614) by the English soldier and author Walter Raleigh, who sponsored expeditions to Virginia. Both books provided support for the Puritans' beliefs in their destiny. Bradstreet wrote an elegy to Du Bartas, and one of her historical poems was inspired by Raleigh.

Other poems in *The Tenth Muse* include "A Dialogue Between Old England and New" (1642) and the elegy "In Honour of Queen Elizabeth" (1643). Bradstreet wrote "A Dialogue" about the 1642 Puritan uprising led by English revolutionary leader Oliver Cromwell against the Royalists (supporters of the monarchy) of King Charles I. In the poem, Bradstreet claimed that until England was rid of Roman Catholicism (a branch of Christianity headed by a pope in Rome, Italy), New England colonists should have no connection with their homeland. "In Honour of Queen Elizabeth" is an example of how Bradstreet constantly challenged the tolerance of the Puritan community. Many men believed that women should not have intellectual interests, especially politics. Bradstreet opposed that line of thinking, and in her elegy she cites the high stature and accomplishments of British queen Elizabeth I as "argument enough to make you mute."

Writes private poetry

After *The Tenth Muse* was published, Bradstreet continued to write poetry. None of these later poems appeared in print in her lifetime, and they have come to be known as her private poems. While *The Tenth Muse* was concerned primarily with history and politics, the private poems are about everyday life in the New World. Because this work is introspective, it reveals deep personal feelings. For instance, the poems about the relationship between Bradstreet and her husband express her love and devotion to him. In 1664 she also began a prose series (nonpoetic work in the language of everyday speech) titled "Meditations Divine and Moral." Written for her son Simon, this work reflects a warm, spirited dimension of Bradstreet that contrasts with the cold Puritan world.

The private poems also reveal that Bradstreet had difficulty submitting to Puritanism. The Puritans believed that

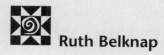

Ruth Belknap

Another well-known colonial American woman poet was Ruth Belknap (dates unknown). Like Bradstreet, Belknap was a member of a privileged family. Being the wife of a minister in Dover, New Hampshire, kept Belknap from being poor. However, like Bradstreet, she still had a difficult life. In her poem "The Pleasures of a Country Life," she described in detail all the chores she had to accomplish as a typical housewife.

> All summer long I toil & sweat,
> Blister my hands, and scold & fret.

> And when the summer's work is o'er,
> New toils arise from Autumn's store.
> Corn must be husk'd, and pork be kill'd.
> The house with all confusion fill'd.
> O could you see the grand display
> Upon our annual butchering day,–
> See me look like ten thousand sluts,
> My kitchen spread with grease & guts.

In the same poem, Belknap goes on to describe the difference between people who live in the country and those who live in town. She portrays the latter as lazy and much less industrious than colonists who were forced to labor on the farm.

every moment spent on earth was merely a preparation for life in Heaven after death. They preferred the wilderness because they believed that the more they suffered in their earthly life, the higher the reward would be in the afterlife. Some of Bradstreet's private poems suggest that she was unhappy in the New World, and she missed the luxury of her previous existence in England. "Contemplations," however, suggests that she was happy in New England. Probably written when the Bradstreet family settled in North Andover in 1645, it was the first poem of the New World to be inspired by the American landscape. In "Contemplations," Bradstreet views nature as a manifestation of God's glory and a symbol of the afterlife. The poem contains almost no classical allusions (references to ancient Greek and Roman literature) like *The Tenth Muse,* and it is a good example of simple Puritan style.

Leaves great legacy

As Bradstreet grew older, she finally became resigned to the will of God. Her last known poem was "As Weary Pilgrim." Written in 1669 and published in 1876, it is evidence that her spiritual struggle was over—Bradstreet says she is anxious to enter the next world. She died in North Andover in 1672, shortly after completing the poem. Bradstreet left behind many works, which were ultimately published. John Foster (who set up the first printing press in Boston) released *Several Poems* (1678), the first American edition of her poetry. Then John Harvard Ellis published *The Works of Anne Bradstreet in Poetry and Prose* (1867). In addition her poetic legacy, Bradstreet also had famous descendants. Among them were abolitionist Wendell Phillips and U.S. Supreme Court Justice Oliver Wendell Holmes.

For further research

"Anne Bradstreet" in *The Puritans: American Literature Colonial Period (1608-1700).* http://falcon.jmu.edu/-ramseyil/amicol.htm Available July 13, 1999.

Dunham, Montrew. *Anne Bradstreet; Young Puritan Poet.* Indianapolis, IN: Bobbs-Merrill, 1969.

James, Edward T., and others, eds. *Notable American Women, 1607–1950,* Volume I. Cambridge, MA: Belknap Press of Harvard University Press, 1971, pp. 222–23.

White, Elizabeth Wade. *Anne Bradstreet, "The Tenth Muse."* New York: Oxford University Press, 1971.

Margaret Brent

c.1601
Gloucester, England
c.1671
Virginia

Landowner and business agent

Margaret Brent was a unique figure in seventeenth-century Maryland. An independent, wealthy woman, she was actively involved in the legal and political affairs of the colony at a time when women had little or no power. Brent is remembered today as a feminist because she demanded the right to vote in Maryland, even though she knew she would be denied the privilege because of her gender. It is believed that she was the first practicing female attorney in America. Some historians point out, however, that Brent was not actually advocating equality for women in general, and she was never licensed as a lawyer. Nonetheless, she was an exceptional woman for her day: she owned and managed a large estate, she was the executor (one appointed to carry out a will) of the Maryland governor's estate, and at one point she managed the supply and payment of an army.

Acquires land in Maryland

Margaret Brent was born around 1601, in Gloucester, England. Her father, Richard Brent, was Lord of Admington and Lark Stoke in the county of Gloucester. Her mother, Eliza-

" . . . it was better for the Collonys safety at the time in her hands then in any mans else in the whole Province. . . . "

The Maryland Assembly.

beth (Reed) Brent, was a descendant of King Edward III. Very little is known about her early life except that she received some education and that she was raised a Roman Catholic (Christian religion based in Rome, Italy, and headed by a pope who is the supreme authority in all church affairs).

On November 22, 1638, Brent emigrated (moved from one country to another) to St. Mary's, the capital of the Maryland colony in North America. She moved there with her sister Mary, her brothers Giles and Fulke, and several servants. Maryland was founded in 1632 by Cecilius Calvert, Second Baron Baltimore (also known as Lord Baltimore), who had received the grant from King Charles II. The Calverts were Roman Catholic, as were many of the Maryland settlers. When the Brents left England, they carried a letter from Cecilius Calvert. Although he was the proprietor (one granted ownership of a colony) of Maryland, he remained in England and governed the colony through deputies (officials representing the proprietor). In his letter Calvert recommended that the Brent family be given land according to the same terms that were granted the first settlers of Maryland. The Brent family, like many other settlers in the New World (a European term for North America and South America), hoped to take advantage of opportunities in the thriving American colonies.

If the Brents were to be afforded the same rights as previous settlers, this meant the Brent sisters would have the same right to own land as men. They were granted 70.5 acres of land in St. Mary's, calling their new property "Sisters Freehold." In 1642 Brent acquired even more land from her brother Giles in return for payment of a debt. She also received land from her brother Fulke. Within a year of arriving in Maryland, Fulke returned to England and bestowed upon his sister full power of attorney (authority to handle legal affairs) over his property. This was only the first of many responsibilities for Brent, who eventually became a highly influential figure in the colony.

Becomes executor of estate

Having obtained power of attorney, Brent now had the authority to represent Fulke in all legal and financial matters concerning his Maryland property. From a historical perspective this may seem unusual because Brent was a woman, and women had only limited freedom during colonial times. Nev-

The Calverts in Maryland

The founding of Maryland began with George Calvert, First Baron Baltimore (also known as Lord Baltimore), who declared himself a Roman Catholic in 1625. He had close ties with the Virginia Company and the New England Company, groups of investors who were starting colonies in North America. Nevertheless, Calvert wanted to found his own settlement. At that time investors were granted charters (titles to land) in North America by the British king or queen. These investors, called proprietors, were permitted to found and govern colonies as private enterprises. In 1623 Calvert was given the peninsula of Avalon in Newfoundland, but because of the extremely cold climate, the colony failed. Six years later, Calvert was granted territory north of the Potomac River on the Atlantic coast in North America. He prepared a charter for a colony, but he died shortly before it was approved. In 1632 his son Cecilius, Second Baron Baltimore, received the charter and founded the colony of Maryland. Cecilius Calvert never visited Maryland himself. Instead, he remained in England. However, he governed through a series of deputies, including his brother Leonard. The last deputy governor of Maryland was Cecilius's son Charles Calvert, Third Baron Baltimore. Charles was sent to govern the colony in 1661 and was appointed proprietor upon the death of Cecilius in 1675.

The Roman Catholic Calverts faced constant opposition from Protestants, who increasingly became the majority of the population in Maryland. Charles Calvert tried to protect Catholic interests by depriving Protestants of the right to vote and by filling offices with his allies. New pressures on the colony resulted from Calvert's dispute with **William Penn** (see entry), the Quaker proprietor of Pennsylvania, over the boundary between Maryland and Pennsylvania. (Quakers are members of the Religious Society of Friends that believe that the individual can receive divine truth from the Holy Spirit through his or her own "inner light" without the guidance of a minister or priest.) In 1684 Calvert traveled to England to defend his position. He found himself charged with favoring Catholics and preventing the collection of taxes on commercial goods. Calvert never returned to Maryland. His charter was overturned during the 1689 Protestant revolt in England. Three years later the royal government of Britain took direct control of the colony.

ertheless, there were very few professional lawyers in Maryland in the 1640s. People who needed legal guidance often represented themselves before the courts. Because there were no strict guidelines determining who could be a lawyer, it was possible for Brent to handle her own legal matters. Of all the amateur lawyers (those not licensed to practice law), she was perhaps the most successful of her day.

While it is clear that the Brent family was influential in Maryland, some historians believe that a large part of this power came from their connections with the Calverts. It was Cecilius Calvert that had granted them their Maryland property. The Brents' power may have been further strengthened when Governor Leonard Calvert married Brent's sister Anne. He was greatly impressed by Brent's actions as an amateur lawyer. She and Leonard Calvert also shared the guardianship (one who has the care of a person) of Mary Kitomaquund, the daughter of the chief of the Piscataway tribe.

Brent had made such an impression on Calvert, in fact, that before he died in 1647 he named her the executor of his will. In this position Brent handled claims made against the late governor's estate and collected debts owed to him. Not only did she assume responsibility for Leonard Calvert's property, but the Maryland court also put her in charge of the estate of Cecilius Calvert. This action made Brent the most powerful woman in the colony and propelled her to the forefront of Maryland politics.

Arranges pay for soldiers

When Brent took over the Calvert estates, Maryland was going through a period of crisis. In 1645 Protestants led by Richard Ingle, an English seaman and tobacco trader, revolted against the Catholic government of the colony. Known as Ingle's Rebellion (1645–47), the uprising lasted for two years. In order to put down the revolt, Leonard Calvert hired soldiers from Virginia and promised to pay them with money raised from the Calvert estates. Unfortunately, Calvert died before he could pay the army of soldiers and Brent was left in charge of reimbursing the men. This was a large responsibility, considering the limited power Brent had as a woman. Calvert could have made Brent's brother Giles the executor of his will, but Giles had been captured during the rebellion and taken to England as a prisoner. He did not return to Maryland until after the governor's death.

As it turned out, Brent was a capable executor. In fact, subsequent events proved her to be highly resourceful. Her

Claiborne Rebellion

The Claiborne Rebellion (1645–47) was led by William Claiborne, who had emigrated to Virginia from England in 1621. He established a settlement with a fort on Kent Island in Chesapeake Bay. Problems arose when he violently opposed the granting of Maryland to Cecilius Calvert, Second Baron Baltimore. (Claiborne was a Protestant, and he did not want his settlement to come under the rule of Calvert, who was a Roman Catholic.) After Claiborne was arrested and sent to England in 1637, he argued his case, but the issue was eventually decided in favor of Calvert. Nevertheless, Claiborne returned to Virginia, and in 1642 he was elected treasurer of the colony. For several years he continued to invade Maryland. After driving out Governor Leonard Calvert, Claiborne briefly gained control of the colony. Although Calvert returned in 1646 and put down the uprising, he died

Portrait: William Claiborne. *Reproduced by permission of Archive Photos, Inc.*

the following year. Claiborne controlled Maryland for several years after Calvert's death and served on the governing commission of the colony.

duties included not only paying the soldiers but also feeding them. In order to accomplish this task, Brent was allowed to use Cecilius Calvert's estate if Leonard's property did not yield enough resources. When a food shortage forced her to import supplies from Virginia, she discovered that Leonard's estate did not have enough money to cover all the expenses. Therefore, she was forced to draw money from Cecilius's estate. Brent then sold off some of the proprietor's cattle in order to pay the soldiers their wages. Although this bold act drew criticism from Cecilius Calvert in England, Brent's handling of the affair preserved order in Maryland after Ingle's Rebellion had been subdued. The new governor, Thomas Greene, was consequently able to make a peaceful transition.

Requests right to vote

During her struggle to provide for the Virginia soldiers, Brent showed considerable abilities. Nevertheless, she continued to be discriminated against because of her gender. Then on January 21, 1647 (or 1648), Brent earned a place in history by asking the Maryland assembly for the right to vote. This power would have enabled her to make decisions equally with landowning men in the colony. She requested two votes: one because she was a landowner (all male landowners were given a vote) and the other because she was the proprietor's attorney. Evidently, Brent believed that if she was exercising so much responsibility she should be granted voting rights. Although Greene denied her request, she was commended by the Maryland assembly for successfully managing the compensation of the Virginia soldiers.

Moves from Maryland to Virginia

In 1651 Brent moved with her family to Virginia, where she acquired a plantation that she named "Peace." Historians cite her gender as the reason for her limited success in Maryland. However, other factors were involved. For instance, Cecilius Calvert was upset that Brent had used his cattle to raise money for the soldiers. Furthermore, because Protestants were gaining power in England, Calvert found it increasingly difficult to support other Roman Catholics like Brent. Her brother Giles also had a negative impact on her position in Maryland because he was a Jesuit (a member of the Roman Catholic Society). Despite these obstacles, Brent did very well for herself. In her will, which she wrote in 1663, she gave up her rights to the land in Maryland. Brent died in Virginia around 1671.

For further research

James, Edward T., and others, eds. *Notable American Women, 1607–1950,* Volume I. Cambridge, MA: Belknap Press of Harvard University Press, 1971, pp. 236–37.

Johnson, Allen, and others, eds. *Dictionary of American Biography.* New York: Scribner, 1946–1958, pp. 18–19.

William Byrd II

March 28, 1674
Richmond, Virginia
August 26, 1744
Westover, Virginia

Planter, colonial official, and writer

William Byrd II was a wealthy landowner and government official in eighteenth-century Virginia. His success in large part came from inheriting one of the largest fortunes of the time. After receiving a gentleman's education in England, Byrd returned to America with great political and social ambitions. Elected to the Council of Virginia in 1709, he was firmly devoted to the political interests of the colony. He successfully battled Lieutenant Governor Alexander Spotswood, who tried to limit the power of the council. Byrd had a reputation as a carouser (one who engages in loose behavior) and a womanizer. Despite these faults, he worked hard, significantly expanding the Byrd estate and rebuilding the great family mansion at Westover plantation.

Educated in England

William Byrd II was born in 1674 in what is now Richmond, Virginia. His father was William Byrd I, and his mother, Mary, was the daughter of Warham Horsmanden. Being the son of William Byrd I meant that someday Byrd would inherit one of the largest fortunes in the late-seventeenth-century Vir-

" . . . like one of the patriarchs, I have my flocks and my herds, my bond-men and bond-women, and every soart [sic] of trade amongst my own servants, so that I live in a kind of independence on every one, but Providence."

William Byrd.

Portrait: William Byrd II.
Reproduced by permission of Archive Photos, Inc.

Robert Beverley, Virginia gentleman

Even though William Byrd II was an unusual individual, he was in some ways similar to other elite Virginia landowners. In fact, he shared several traits with one of his contemporaries, Robert Beverley. Like Byrd, Beverley was educated in England, had inherited great wealth, and served in Virginia government. After being elected to the House of Burgesses (the governing body of the Virginia colony) around 1700, Beverley, like Byrd, supported Virginia in conflicts with England. He even married Byrd's sister Ursula, although she died within a year and Beverley never remarried.

Both men were also writers. Beverley was an author of books on Virginia. His best work, *The History and Present State of Virginia* (1705), was first published anonymously. If Beverley and Byrd differed in any way, it was that Beverley had a more moderate nature. In his book he did not romanticize the New World; instead, he portrayed it as a place that had to be developed through hard work. Yet *The History and Present State of Virginia* was also intended to lure Europeans to Virginia. In promoting Virginia as a beautiful colony, Beverley glossed over the violence of such events as Bacon's Rebellion of 1676 (see **Nathaniel Bacon** entry). His other work was a legal text, *An Abridgement of the Public Laws of Virginia* (1722).

ginia. The elder Byrd had inherited vast land holdings in America, along with lucrative (producing wealth) interests in the rum, slave, tobacco, and fur trades. He also had a seat on the Virginia governor's council. This was a position of great influence that could be exploited to gain more wealth.

Despite their social position in Virginia, however, life on a frontier plantation still had its challenges for the Byrd family. William Byrd I feared the influence that African American slaves, who performed the physical labor on the plantation, might have on his son. Therefore, the younger Byrd was sent to be educated in England when he was only seven years old. During his young years he received some of the best training that England had to offer in business, literature, and law. In 1684 he studied the classics (literature of ancient Greece and Rome) and modern languages with a leading schoolmaster named Christopher Glassock in Essex. In 1690 Byrd traveled to Holland to learn business at the great merchant houses. In 1692 he began his legal training at the renowned Middle Temple in London, England. Byrd also toured the European continent, another essential element of an English gentleman's education.

During his years in London, Byrd socialized with important political and cultural figures in drawing rooms, coffeehouses, and theaters. In the process he made friends and acquired contacts that would make the Byrd name known and respected in England. Among his closest and most important friends were two men of science, Robert Boyle, Earl of Orrery, and Robert Southwell. With their help Byrd gained admission to the Royal Society at the age of twenty-two. In 1696 he and **Cotton Mather**(see entry) were the only two American members of the distinguished scientific organization. This honor, along with his English education and social connections, made Byrd an influential figure, both in England and Virginia.

Serves in Council of Virginia

After many years abroad, Byrd returned to Virginia. He was elected to the House of Burgesses in 1692. When he was admitted to the bar (the profession of lawyer) in 1695—a distinction few Englishmen at the time attained—he traveled back to England and defended the British governor of Virginia, Edmund Andros, who was being charged with hostility against the Anglican Church of Virginia. In 1704, after his father died, Byrd returned to Virginia to claim his fortune and take his place among the colony's leaders. Because Byrd had spent most of his life in England, it was uncertain whether or not he would fit in with colonial Americans. However, as it turned out, his education and personality made him more than compatible with the elite group of men ruling Virginia at the time. Byrd devoted the next eleven years to enlarging Westover, climbing the social ladder, and raising a family.

In 1706 Byrd married Lucy Parke, the daughter of General Daniel Parke, a leading Virginian who became governor of the Leeward Islands. Despite their wealth and privilege, the couple had a difficult marriage. For instance, two of their four children died in early childhood. They also frequently quarreled over Byrd's conduct with other women and his manage-

Alexander Spotswood

Alexander Spotswood, the man who tried to oust William Byrd II from the Council of Virginia, was born in Tangier, Morocco. He began serving as lieutenant governor of Virginia in 1710, under the governorship of George Hamilton. At first Spotswood was a popular leader, but his support soon began to decline as he took on several controversial issues. In addition to attempting to limit the power of the council, he required the inspection of tobacco in 1713 and regulated trade with Native Americans the following year. In 1722 he negotiated a treaty with the Iroquois Indians that forced them to remain beyond the Potomac River and the Blue Ridge Mountains. It is believed that this treaty might have been an effort on behalf of settlers to push Native Americans farther west. At the end of his governorship in 1722, Spotswood retired to his estate in Spotsylvania County, the future site of many battles during the American Civil War (1861–65).

Alexander Spotswood. *Reproduced by Permission of the Library of Congress.*

ment of the plantation slaves. Because domestic misconduct was common among Virginia planters at the time, Byrd actually earned respect for this behavior. In fact, he so impressed his contemporaries with his business sense and social abilities that after being elected to council in 1709, he was appointed the Virginia colonial agent in London in 1715. Because of his new position, Byrd then traveled to London to represent Virginia's economic and political interests before Parliament (the supreme legislative body in England). Lucy died of smallpox shortly after his arrival, and Byrd remained in London for more than a decade.

Preserves power of the council

In 1710, Alexander Spotswood arrived in Virginia from England to begin serving as lieutenant governor. It did not take long for Spotswood to come into conflict with the Council of Virginia, which consisted of wealthy landowners like Byrd. While in office, Spotswood tried to limit the power of the council, thereby making himself highly unpopular with the council members in the colony. First he attempted to limit the council's ability to monopolize (assume complete possession or control of) vast areas of land by collecting quit-rents (a fixed rent payable to a feudal superior in exchange for services). Byrd and his colleagues fiercely protested this action. Second, Spotswood proposed a reform of judicial power of the council, which had served as the supreme court in Virginia for many decades. He wanted to devise a new system that would not contain any council members.

While Byrd was in England, he brought the concerns of the Council of Virginia before the Board of Trade, which regulated commerce in English colonies. He claimed that Spotswood's having absolute control over both the economic and legal systems of the colony would be a serious threat to the freedom of Virginians. Spotswood argued that, to the contrary, the English king must retain power over Virginia. Therefore, the majority of that power must be given to the governor, not the council, which presently had too much control. Finally, in 1718, Spotswood tried to have Byrd permanently removed from the council. When Byrd arrived in Virginia in 1720 with orders to resolve the problem, Spotswood was removed instead. This left the council intact, with continued power over the colony of Virginia.

Writes books about exploration

After spending many years in England as a widower, Byrd married Maria Tyler in 1724. Two years later he returned to Virginia permanently. In his later years, Byrd continued serving on the Council of Virginia. Shortly before he died he was elected council president. He was also receiver-general of Crown revenues, a lucrative post as overseer of the collection of customs (taxes), a job that his father had held. However, despite his great wealth, Byrd was frequently in debt. In order to pay creditors, he often had to sell land and slaves. Eventu-

William Byrd's "secret history"

Throughout his life William Byrd kept a personal diary (published as *Secret History* in 1929). It provides a detailed picture of the life of an eighteenth-century Virginia gentleman. Excerpted below is Byrd's account of his daily routine at his Virginia plantation. The entries show that Byrd observed a strict schedule of reading and prayer, yet he also engaged in activities that earned him a reputation as a carouser and womanizer.

[IN VIRGINIA, JUNE 1720]

20. I rose about 5 o'clock and read a chapter in Hebrew and some Greek. I said my prayers, and had boiled milk for breakfast. The weather continued very hot. However, about 8 o'clock I went to Mrs. Harrison's in a boat and ate some milk there. We played at piquet [a card game] and shot with bows and I won five bits [small coins]. Sometimes we romped [had fun] and sometimes talked and complained of the heat till dinner and then I ate some hashed lamb. After dinner we romped again and drank abundance of water. We played at piquet again and I stayed till 8 o'clock and then took leave and walked home and found everything well, thank God. I talked with my people and said my prayers and then retired and slept but indifferently because of the exceedingly great heat.

21. I rose about 5 o'clock and read a chapter in Hebrew and some Greek. I neglected to say my prayers, but had milk for breakfast. The weather continued very hot and we began to cut down our wheat. About 9 o'clock came Frank Lightfoot and we played at billiards [pool] and then at piquet and I won two bits. Then we sat and talked till dinner when I ate some beans and bacon. After dinner we agreed to take a nap and slept about an hour and then I received a letter from New Kent that told me William R-s-t-n [a slave] was run away. Then Mr. Lightfoot and I played again at piquet till the evening and then walked about the garden till night and then he went away and I gave my people a bowl of punch and they had a fiddle and danced and I walked in the garden till ten and then committed uncleanness [engaged in sexual intercourse] with Annie. I said my prayers.

ally he managed to earn back much that he had lost. In 1728, while serving as a commissioner, Byrd headed a team of surveyors (those who measure and describe the geographic characteristics of a tract of land) from Virginia and North Carolina in establishing a boundary line between the two colonies. He also surveyed the Northern Neck region of Virginia in 1736. Service on behalf of Virginia helped Byrd gain more land. By the time of his death, he had turned the 26,000-acre Westover Plantation he had inherited from his father into almost 180,000 acres.

In addition to being a councilman and a landowner, Byrd was a writer. His diaries were published as *Secret History* in 1929. This work revealed some of the misconduct that Byrd was famous for as a public figure. One of his major works, "The History of the Dividing Line," was an account of his 1728 expedition to survey the Virginia–North Carolina boundary. He wrote this piece, which contrasted with his personal diaries, in a style that captured the colonial American spirit of exploration. "The History of the Dividing Line" was first published along with "A Journey to the Land of Eden" and "Progress to the Mines" as *The Westover Manuscripts* in 1841. These works, while presenting Byrd as an adventurous well-rounded public figure, also served as a model for other authors of exploration literature in years to come.

Byrd mansion still stands

Not surprisingly, Byrd's wealth depended in great measure on his slaves, which in 1718 included well over 200 men and women located on several plantations. With Byrd managing the job, some of the skilled "tradesmen" among the African American slaves rebuilt the great Byrd family home at Westover on the James River into a red-brick Georgian mansion surrounded by English gardens. Byrd also built a great library with more than 3,000 volumes, rivaling the collection held by Cotton Mather. Because the Byrd mansion was a place of solitude and beauty, it is considered a predecessor to Monticello, the mansion built in 1772 by the American statesman Thomas Jefferson. After spending his last few years living on his estate, Byrd died on August 26, 1744. Unfortunately, William Byrd III, a son from his second marriage, gambled away most of the family fortune. The Byrd mansion still stands, however, as a fine example of colonial American architecture.

For further research

Elliott, Emory, and others, eds. *American Literature: A Prentice Hall Anthology.* Englewood Cliffs, New Jersey: Prentice Hall, 1991, pp. 245–46.

Johnson, Allen, and others, eds. *Dictionary of American Biography.* New York: Scribner, 1946–1958, p. 383.

Lockridge, Kenneth A. *The Diary, and Life, of William Byrd II of Virginia, 1674–1744.* Chapel Hill: University of North Carolina Press, 1987.

"William Byrd II." http://marist.chi.il.us/_amlit/laurph2.html Available July 13, 1999.

Jacques Cartier

December 31, 1491
Saint-Malo, France
September 1, 1557
Saint-Malo, France

French explorer

> " . . . the said unknown sickness began to spread itself amongst us after the strangest sort that ever was either heard of or seen. . . . "
>
> *Jacques Cartier.*

Portrait: Jacques Cartier.
Reproduced by permission of Archive Photos, Inc.

J acques Cartier was a French explorer who made three voyages to Canada during the mid-sixteenth century. His expeditions were inspired by the belief that a natural waterway leading to Asia could be found through the continents of North America and South America. At the time, numerous explorers searched for this route, which became known as the Northwest Passage. During his first voyage, in 1534, Cartier explored the Gulf of St. Lawrence. After the second voyage, a trip up the St. Lawrence River in 1535, he returned to France and claimed that the river could be the passage to Asia. In 1541 the king of France ordered Cartier to establish a colony in North America. His attempts were unsuccessful, however, and France did not explore the New World (a European term for North America and South America) again for more than fifty years.

Sent to find gold

Jacques Cartier was born in 1491 in the port of Saint-Malo in the province of Brittany in France. Little is known about his early life, but it is clear that he made several sea voyages. According to some accounts, he may have been a crew member on two expeditions to America led by the Italian explorer **Giovanni da Verrazano** (see entry) in 1524 and 1528. In 1532 the bishop of Saint-Malo proposed to King François I of France that the king sponsor an expedition to the New World and that Cartier lead it. To sway the king, the bishop pointed out that Cartier had already been to Brazil and the island of Newfoundland. After François I approved the nomination on April 20, 1534, Cartier set off from Saint-Malo with two ships and sixty-one men. His mission was "to discover certain islands and lands where it is said that a great quantity of gold, and other precious things, are to be found." From the outset it was clear that Cartier was expected to find mineral wealth, such as gold and silver.

Jacques Cartier claiming land for France during his exploration of the Gulf of St. Lawrence. *Reproduced by permission of the Library of Congress.*

Explores Gulf of St. Lawrence

Cartier's fleet sailed to the northern tip of Newfoundland, and entered the Strait of Belle Isle, which was known to lead to open waters beyond. In order to avoid the barren northern coast, Cartier headed south along the western shore of Newfoundland, naming many rivers and harbors. The party continued along the western coast until they came to the channel, now called Cabot Strait, that connects the Gulf of St. Lawrence with the Atlantic Ocean. Since Cartier did not enter Cabot Strait, he did not discover that it separates Newfoundland from Cape Breton Island and thus provides a better route for entering the Gulf of St. Lawrence than the Strait of Belle Isle.

In the course of exploring the Gulf of St. Lawrence, Cartier was the first European to report on the Magdalen Islands (Iles de la Madeleine) and Prince Edward Island. His party then sailed on to the coast of New Brunswick, where he explored Chaleur Bay. Heading north along the coast to Gaspé Bay, he claimed the Gaspé Peninsula for France. From Gaspé, Cartier continued to Anticosti Island, but he did not travel far enough beyond Anticosti to discover the St. Lawrence River. After he went ashore to claim the land for France, he encountered the Iroquois chief Donnacona. When Cartier left, he took two of the chief's sons with him as guests (some historians say as prisoners) on the return trip to France.

Begins second voyage

Upon his arrival in Saint-Malo on September 5, 1534, Cartier received a hero's welcome. Although he had not found any gold, he brought reports of a warm climate and fertile land in New Brunswick and the Gaspé Peninsula. The region had previously been considered suitable for fishing but certainly not for settlement and commercial trade. Intrigued by Cartier's report, the king planned a second voyage. The following year he provided Cartier with three ships for a return trip to Canada. Cartier left Saint-Malo on May 15, 1535, taking with him Donnacona's two sons, who had learned French in order to serve as translators.

This proved to be Cartier's most important voyage. Guided by the Iroquois, he sailed west from Anticosti and, on August 13, entered the great estuary (a water passage) of the St. Lawrence. The river would become the main gateway for French exploration in North America for the next two centuries. Cartier sailed up the St. Lawrence past the Saguenay River to the village of Stadacona, on the site of present-day Quebec City. After meeting with Donnacona he traveled farther up the river to the village of Hochelaga, where the city of Montreal is now located. When Cartier encountered dangerous rapids, he ordered the ships not to travel any farther. He was informed by the Iroquois, however, that the St. Lawrence River extended further west to a region where gold and silver could be found.

Describes epidemic

During his stay in Canada, Cartier climbed Mount Royal to view the St. Lawrence valley. He also saw the Lachine Rapids and the Ottawa River. After planting a cross at Hochelaga, Cartier's party returned to Stadacona in October, where they settled for the winter. Cartier and his men were the first Europeans to spend the winter in Canada, and they were surprised at the extreme cold. Despite growing tension between the French and the Iroquois, the Native people helped Cartier's party survive an epidemic of scurvy (a disease caused by a lack of vitamin C). In February 1536, Cartier wrote an account of the difficult winter, describing the rapid decline of his men:

In the month of December we understood that the pestilence [a devastating contagious epidemic disease] was come among the people of Stadacona [the Iroquois], in such sort that before we knew it, according to their confession, there were dead above 50; whereupon we charged them neither to come near our fort, nor about our ships, or us. And albeit [even though] we had driven them from us, the said unknown sickness began to spread itself amongst us after the strangest sort that ever was either heard of or seen, insomuch as some did lose all their strength and could not stand on their feet; then did their legs swell, their sinews [tendons] shrink as black as any coal. Others also had all their skins spotted with spots of blood of a purple colour; then did it ascend up to their ankles, knees, thighs, shoulders, arms, and neck; their mouth became stinking, their gums so rotten that all the flesh did fall off, even to the roots of the teeth, which did also almost all fall out.

Cartier's report continued:

With such infection did this sickness spread itself in our three ships that about the middle of February, of 110 persons that we were, there were not ten whole, so that one could not help the other—a most horrible and pitiful case. As more men died, an autopsy was ordered on twenty-two-year-old Philip Rougemont, in the hope of finding a cure. Rougemont was found to have his heart white but rotten and more than a quart of red water about it; his liver was indifferent fair, but his lungs black and mortified; his blood was altogether shrunk about the heart so that, when he was opened, a great quantity of rotten blood issued out from about his heart.

This chilling account is only one example of the terrible symptoms that all of the scurvy victims of the Cartier party experienced that winter.

Iroquois provide cure

Fortunately, there was good news for the sick men. Cartier met with the Iroquois and remarked at how one of them, a man named Domagaia, appeared to be cured of the disease. When questioned, Domagaia responded "that he had taken the juice and sap of the leaves of a certain tree and therewith had healed himself, for it is a singular remedy against that disease." The cure consisted of the bark and leaves of the Iroquois ameda tree (possibly a sassafras tree), boiled together and consumed every other day. After cutting down a huge tree, the Frenchmen were able to prepare enough of the remedy to cure all of their men. Cartier remarked on the effectiveness of the simple cure, observing that all the doctors in the modern world could not "have done so much in one year as that tree did in six days."

Embarks on final voyage

When Cartier left Stadacona for France on May 6, 1536, he took Donnacona with him. They arrived in France on July 16. Cartier's second voyage had been a great success. He had found a major waterway that might be the sought-after route to Asia, and he even brought back a few pieces of gold. François wanted to send Cartier back to Canada immediately. But war broke out between France and the Holy Roman Empire, so Cartier was unable to leave the country. In the meantime, the rights to colonize Canada had been granted to a French nobleman, Jean-François de La Rocque, Sieur de Roberval. Cartier was assigned to return and gather information for Roberval's voyage the following year.

The expedition reached Stadacona on August 23, 1541. Donnacona had died in France, but his death probably made it easier for Cartier to deal with Donnacona's successor, Agona, who now did not have to worry about his rival. While building a camp at the present-day town of Charlesbourg, north of Quebec, Cartier found some minerals he thought were diamonds. After making a brief trip back to Hochelaga, he returned to spend the winter at Charlesbourg. Once again the Frenchmen suffered through a harsh winter. They were also faced with the growing hostility of the Iroquois, so in the spring Cartier and his party decided to head back to France.

Cartier's party left Stadacona in June 1542 and traveled to the port of St. John's, Newfoundland. During the entire trip Cartier had not seen Roberval, but the two men finally met as Cartier was preparing to sail. Cartier received instructions to return to Canada with Roberval and help him found the new colony. However, in the dark of night he and his men slipped away and sailed for France, leaving Roberval to fend for himself. When Cartier arrived back in Saint-Malo, he found himself in a lot of trouble. The "gold" he was carrying was discovered to really be iron pyrite and the "diamonds" were quartz crystals. Furthermore, Cartier had once again failed to explore far enough up the St. Lawrence River because of the dangerous rapids. Finally, when Roberval returned without settling a new colony, the king was disappointed. The French did not explore the New World again for more than fifty years.

Spends final years in France

Cartier is one of the best-known explorers in North American history. However, historians cite three factors that diminish his stature. First, he failed to thoroughly explore the St. Lawrence River. It is believed that he could easily have sailed beyond the rapids at Hochelaga and made his way to Lake Ontario and possibly Lake Erie. Second, Cartier is criticized for his dealings with the Iroquois. It is debatable whether he took Donnacona and his sons back to France as guests or as prisoners. Finally, his conduct toward Roberval is questionable. Even though he was not punished for leaving Roberval behind, Cartier was never again granted a commission by France. Cartier spent his remaining years in Saint-Malo as a prosperous businessman. His book about his second voyage to Newfoundland was published in 1545. Cartier died in Saint-Malo on September 1, 1557.

For further research

Coulter, Tony, and William H. Goetzmann, eds. *Jacques Cartier, Samuel de Champlain and the Explorers of Canada.* New York: Chelsea House Publishers, 1993.

"Jacques Cartier." http://www.win.tue.nl/cs/fm/engels/discovery/cartier.html Available July 13, 1999.

Morison, Samuel Eliot. *The Great Explorers: The European Discovery of America.* New York: Oxford University Press, 1986.

Trudel, Marcel. "Jacques Cartier." *Dictionary of Canadian Biography,* Volume 1. Toronto: University of Toronto Press, 1967.

Samuel de Champlain

c. 1567
Brouage, France
December 25, 1635
Quebec, New France (now Canada)

French explorer

I n 1608 the French explorer Samuel de Champlain visited New France, a French colony in North America that became the province of Quebec, Canada. Within four years he had convinced the French government that the land in North America had great potential for settlement and commercial development. Champlain made twelve journeys to New France to explore and consolidate French holdings in the New World (a European term for North and South America). He wrote six books about his expeditions and the importance of the new French settlement. Serving for a time as the king's lieutenant in New France, he lived to see Quebec established on both shores of the St. Lawrence River. Today Champlain is considered the father of New France and the founder of Quebec.

Becomes a navigator

Samuel de Champlain was born in the small seaport town of Brouage on the west coast of France in about 1567. It is believed that he was born a Protestant and at some point converted to Roman Catholicism during the Wars of Religion (also known as Hugenot Wars; 1562–98). This period of bitter rivalry between Protestants (members of the Protestant Christian religion, which was formed in opposition to the Roman Catholic Church) and Catholics (members of the Roman Catholic Church, a Christian religion based in Rome, Italy, and headed by a pope who has supreme authority in all church affairs) would determine the dominant religion in France. At an early age, Champlain went to sea to learn navigation and cartography (the drafting of maps and charts). Until 1598 he fought as a sergeant on the side of Protestant king Henry IV in the religious wars. After his military service, he worked as a navigator on a voyage to the West Indies. Although Champlain was born a commoner (one who is not of noble rank), his reputation as a navigator earned him an honorary title in Henry's court.

Joins expedition to New France

In 1603 Champlain was invited to join the expedition of François Gravé Du Pont to visit the river of Canada, now known as the St. Lawrence River. The expedition party landed at Tadoussac, a summer trading post where the Saguenay River runs into the St. Lawrence. Champlain sailed with the expedition past the sites of present-day Quebec, Trois-Rivières, and Montreal. He immediately realized that these lands could be colonized by French citizens and provide France with many resources and great wealth. Champlain also learned of the existence of the Great Lakes. The French found the land sparsely inhabited by Native Americans, some of whom were friendly toward the Europeans while others were hostile. Champlain wrote about the customs of the Native Americans in a report that was published in France.

Returning to Tadoussac, the expedition sailed around the Gaspé Peninsula into a region Champlain called Acadia (probably named for Arcadia, the mythical paradise of the ancient Greeks). Champlain urged the French government to explore Acadia, now known as Nova Scotia. The region reportedly had rich mineral deposits and some speculated it might even be the key to finding the elusive Northwest Passage (the water route between the Atlantic and Pacific Oceans that the major world powers had long been seeking).

As a result of his impressive efforts in New France, Champlain was chosen in 1604 to be the geographer on an

Samuel de Champlain and his crew arrange to cross a river during his exploration of New England.
Reproduced by permission of the Library of Congress.

expedition to Acadia to find the best site for settlement. Led by Lieutenant-General Pierre du Gua, Sieur de Monts, who had a monopoly (exclusive possession or control) on the fur trade in the region, the party of settlers sailed to Acadia. Traveling down the coast of New Brunswick, they stopped at the St. Croix River and built a small fort on a site that is now almost exactly on the border between the United States and Canada. The first winter was a near disaster for the expedition party. Besides the harsh weather, nearly half the party died of scurvy (a disease caused by lack of Vitamin C in the diet). The following winter they moved across the Bay of Fundy to Port Royal, now called Annapolis Royal in Nova Scotia. This was to become the main settlement for the French Acadians.

Explores present-day New England

During the next three years Champlain traveled on his own, trying to find an ideal site for colonization. He sailed along the coast of present-day Maine and journeyed as far as 150 miles inland. On another trip, he sailed down the coast of New England to the island that is now Martha's Vineyard, off Cape Cod. Although the English were exploring in the same area and eventually established the Plymouth Colony in 1620, Champlain was the first European to give a detailed account of the region. He is also credited with discovering Mount Desert Island as well as most of the major rivers in Maine.

Since the French could not find a suitable area for settlement, they returned to Acadia to build a more permanent fort at Port Royal. De Monts returned to France and Champlain stayed with the settlers in Acadia. In September 1606, he made another journey to the south as far as the present-day state of Rhode Island. During the following winter the French made the best of their isolated situation by forming the Order of Good Cheer, which sponsored banquets and games and amateur shows. In 1607, when Henry IV canceled de Monts's trading privileges, the entire colony was forced to return to France. Before he left the New World, Champlain had accurately charted the Atlantic coast from the Bay of Fundy to Cape Cod.

Founds Quebec City

Champlain was determined to return to New France, this time on his own terms. By 1608 he had secured financial backing for his most ambitious project in the New World, the beginning of a permanent settlement at Quebec City. Arriving in July, the party, which included thirty-two colonists, built a fort and faced their first hard winter. Only nine people survived to welcome the reinforcements who arrived in June of the following year. That spring, Champlain continued his exploration of Canada by traveling up the St. Lawrence and Richelieu Rivers to a lake that now bears his name, Lake Champlain. In 1609 he joined the Huron tribe and their allies in a great battle against a marauding (raiding) band of Iroquois on Lake Champlain near present-day Crown Point, New York. The French and Hurons defeated the Iroquois, thus beginning 150 years of hostilities between the French and the Iroquois, one of the most powerful tribal nations in North America.

Named lieutenant in New France

In 1612 Champlain returned to France. On the basis of his report, the king decided to make Quebec the center for French fur trading in North America. Champlain provided an account of this meeting in *Voyages of Samuel de Champlain, 1604–1618* (published by Scribner, 1907). He wrote:

> I reported to him in detail all that had transpired in regard to the winter quarters and our new explorations, and my hopes for the future in view of the promises of the savages called Ochasteguins [Hurons] . . . . After I had concluded my interview with His Majesty, Sieur de Monts determined to go to Rouen to meet his associates. . . . They resolved to continue the settlement, and finish the explorations up the great river St. Lawrence, in accordance with the promises of the Ochasteguins.

Around the time of his meeting with the king, Champlain married Hélène Broullé, the daughter of the secretary to the king's chamber. During the next few years, he frequently traveled back and forth between Quebec and France. While in New France he pursued further exploration and tried to nurture the colony in Quebec, but the many political intrigues

Champlain describes torture

In his *Voyages of Samuel de Champlain, 1604–1618* Champlain provides a detailed account of the aftermath of the successful battle the Hurons and their allies waged against the Iroquois in 1609. He describes the torture of an Iroquois prisoner by the Hurons, a common practice among Native Americans in the seventeenth century. As the Hurons proceed to torture the man, Champlain lists the various techniques they used, including branding, scalping, and mutilation. Champlain admits that it was difficult to watch another human being suffer, but he also describes with admiration the strength of the victim who displayed "such firmness that one would have said, at times, that he suffered hardly any pain at all." Evidently it was customary among

warriors on both sides to resist displaying any reaction to pain.

When Champlain turned his back on the torture, the Hurons allowed him to kill the prisoner by shooting him with a musket. Afterwards, they performed perform ritualistic mutilations of the dead body that included cutting off the head, legs, and arms. Champlain explains that following the ritual "we set out on our return with the rest of the prisoners, who kept singing as they went along, with no better hopes for the future than he had had who was so wretchedly treated." Despite his feelings about the brutal spectacle, Champlain concludes his account by saying that when the French, Iroquois, and Hurons went their separate ways, they parted "with loud protestations of mutual friendship."

(secret schemes) in France demanded all his diplomatic skills and much of his time and energy. For example, when the fur trade faltered, he had to muster support for the colony. He came out of this skirmish the victor, having been made a lieutenant in New France by the new king, Louis XIII.

When Champlain returned to Canada in 1613, he explored the Ottawa River to present-day Allumette Island, opening the route that was to become the main river route to the Great Lakes for the next two centuries. By this time the French had made favorable treaties with many Native American tribes, and the fur trade prospered. Champlain then turned his attention to other aspects of governing the colony.

In 1615 he returned from France with the first Roman Catholic missionaries, who came to convert the Native Americans to Christianity. During that summer he saw the Great Lakes for the first time.

Position threatened by politics

The Iroquois presented a real danger to the French colonists. When the French, allied with the Hurons and Algonquins, unsuccessfully attacked an Iroquois stronghold at a site in what is now modern-day New York, Champlain was seriously wounded. He spent the winter recuperating among the Huron people. When he returned to France in 1616, he found that political intrigues at court had once again weakened his position, and he lost the rank of lieutenant in New France. In order to regain what he had lost, he proposed an ambitious plan to colonize Quebec, establish agriculture, and search for the Northwest Passage. He gained the king's support and spent part of 1618 in Quebec.

Champlain's problems in France, however, were not yet over. Plagued by lawsuits and political intrigue, he again appealed to the king to keep his power. This time Champlain was appointed commander of the colony and spent the following years trying to strengthen New France. His authority strengthened when the most powerful man in the French government, Cardinal de Richelieu, formed the company of One Hundred Associates to rule New France with Champlain in charge.

Quebec becomes stable

In 1629 Quebec was attacked and forced to surrender to a party of English privateers (sailors on a private ship transporting goods). Champlain was exiled to England, where he spent the next four years defending the importance of New France and writing accounts of his life. When a peace treaty was signed between England and France in 1632, Champlain was restored to his former post and returned to New France. In 1634 he sent Jean Nicolet, a French trapper and trader, to the west to extend French claims in the region that is now Wisconsin. Westward expansion was made possible through Champlain's friendly relationship with the Hurons. Even

Jean Nicolet makes peace with the Winnebago tribe

Jean Nicolet was a Frenchman who had been living among the Huron, Algonquin, and Nipissing tribes since 1618, working as a trapper and trader. In 1634 French explorer Samuel de Champlain sent Nicolet on a diplomatic mission to the Winnebago tribe, living on the shores of Green Bay in the present-day state of Wisconsin. Because the Winnebagos were enemies of the Algonquins, it was feared that they would trade with the English instead of the French. Since it was believed that the route to the Great Lakes might also lead to China, Nicolet wore an embroidered Chinese robe.

Nicolet began his journey in July 1634 and traveled via the Ottawa River, Lake Nipissing, and the French River to Lake Huron, where he passed through the straits of Michilimackinac to Lake Michigan, then proceeded down to Green Bay. He was the first European to follow this route, which eventually became the passage for French fur traders to the west. One of the great scenes of North American exploration is Nicolet coming ashore in Green Bay dressed in his Chinese robe. Impressing the tribesmen with his elaborate costume, Nicolet successfully completed his mission by signing a peace treaty between the Winnebagos and the French.

though southward movement was still impossible because of the British, Quebec was a stable French settlement. It was stronger, in fact, than the English settlement of Jamestown, in the modern-day state of Virginia (see **John Smith** entry). This progress was the result of Champlain's success as an explorer and diplomat. Having suffered from various health problems since 1633, Champlain died in Quebec on December 25, 1635.

For further research

Armstrong, Joe C. W. *Champlain.* Toronto: Macmillan of Canada, 1987.

Champlain, Samuel de. *Voyages of Samuel de Champlain.* W. L. Grant, ed. New York: Barnes and Noble, 1952.

Morison, Samuel Eliot. *Samuel de Champlain, Father of New France.* Boston, MA: Little, Brown, 1972.

"Samuel de Champlain's 1607 Map." http://lcweb.locgov/exhibits/trea-sures/trr009.html Available July 13, 1999.

Jane Colden

March 27, 1724
New York City
March 10, 1766
Unknown

American botanist

Botanist Jane Colden was America's first great woman scientist. Having grown up on an estate in the New York countryside, Colden was exposed to nature at an early age. She was trained by her father, Cadwallader Colden, who was active in politics and had a strong interest in science. He began teaching his daughter about science after observing her natural inclination toward botany (a branch of biology dealing with plant life). Colden quickly mastered botany techniques as well as the system of plant classification devised by Swedish botanist Carolus Linnaeus. She soon rose to the top of the scientific community and carried on correspondences with many well-known botanists. By the time Colden settled into domestic life after marrying in 1759, she had already established a reputation that far surpassed any expectations for colonial American women.

Begins studying botany

Jane Colden was born on March 27, 1724, in New York City. Both her parents, who were Scottish immigrants, came from respected and well-educated families. Her mother, Alice

> "[Jane Colden] is perhaps the only lady that has so perfectly studied your system. She deserves to be celebrated."
>
> *English botanist Peter Collinson to Swedish botanist Carolus Linnaeus.*

Cadwallader Colden. His love of science was passed on to his daughter Jane.
Reproduced by permission of the Library of Congress.

(Christie) Colden, was the daughter of a clergyman. Her father, Cadwallader Colden, graduated from the University of Edinburgh in Scotland, where he studied medicine. His love of science was a major influence on his daughter. Cadwallader settled in Philadelphia, Pennsylvania, in 1710 and then moved to New York City in 1718. He held a variety of government positions, including surveyor general, acting governor, and member of the council of the Province of New York.

Although Cadwallader was active in politics throughout his life, his main interest was the study of science. Therefore, when Colden was four years old, Cadwallader moved his family to Coldengham estate, which was located just outside Newburgh, New York. He then devoted his attention to science, mainly the study of botany. Jane Colden, who was educated at home, showed a natural inclination toward the study of botany as well. Her father noticed that she liked to read and that she was particularly interested in the family garden. When Jane was twenty-five, Cadwallader trained her as a botanist.

One of the major contributions Cadwallader made to his daughter's training was having her read "Explication of the Principles of Botany," a translation of the work of Linnaeus. As a result, she learned the English translations of many Latin botanical terms and quickly mastered the Linnaean system of plant classification. While her skills as a botanist progressed, she learned to sketch plants and to make ink impressions of leaves. Colden also mastered English descriptions of plants, and by 1757 she had compiled a catalogue of almost four hundred local plants.

Corresponds with important botanists

Colden became a botanist at a time when there was considerable scientific activity throughout the world. Cadwallader was so impressed with his daughter's abilities that he introduced her to the great botanists of America and Europe. A common practice among botanists at the time was to trade plant samples overseas. During the 1750s, Jane Colden corre-

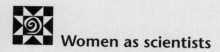

Women as scientists

Jane Colden was considered America's first great woman scientist. She was also one of the few female scientists of her day. If the attitude of her father, Cadwallader Colden, is any indication, it would have been difficult for a woman to pursue an interest in science at the time. Cadwallader was a government official for the Province of New York and an active botanist. Although he regarded women as incapable of rigorous scientific study, he did, however, believe that women could become botanists. He held the almost stereotypical view that women had natural-born ability to recognize beauty, and that they were sympathetic and nurturing. Therefore, he reasoned, women could at least make a limited contribution to serious fields such as medicine, which at the time was heavily influenced by botany.

After Cadwallader taught his daughter botany, he was surprised at her considerable abilities. As part of Jane's training, Cadwallader translated the work of Swedish botanist Carolus Linnaeus. Jane mastered the rigid Linnaean system of plant classification so perfectly that she impressed the entire elite community of botanists. She even collaborated with her father on one of his botanical studies. Cadwallader's attitude toward women is evident in his advice to his daughter Elizabeth: "You have been a Dutyfull Child to your Parents. . . . Let your Dress, your Conversation, and the whole Business of your life be to please your husband and to make him happy." As a rule, this was all that most women could strive for during the colonial period.

sponded with major botanists, including John Ellis and Peter Collinson in London and Charles Alston and Robert Whytt in Edinburgh. She even corresponded with J. F. Gronovius and the great botanist Linnaeus, who had been her primary inspiration. She actually met American naturalist Alexander Garden when he visited Coldengham. She also met American botanists John and William Bartram (see **John Bartram** entry) when they stopped by the estate during their expedition of the Catskill Mountains.

Colden was highly respected by these important botanists. In their own correspondences, they constantly praised her work. For instance, Garden, who considered her work "extreamly accurate," wrote to Ellis on March 25, 1755:

"not only the doctor himself [Cadwallader] is a great botanist, but his lovely daughter is greatly master of the Linnaen method, and cultivates it with assiduity [diligence]." On April 25, 1758, Ellis even suggested to Linnaeus that he label a new plant "Coldenella" as a tribute to her. Even though Linnaeus had already named the plant, he still offered praise for Colden's work. Colden herself was the first scientist to describe the gardenia, which she named after Garden.

Pursues domestic life

On March 12, 1759, Colden married William Farquhar, a Scotsman who practiced medicine in New York City. A friend of Garden, Farquhar knew some of the Scottish botanists who had corresponded with his wife. While there are few records of Colden's personal life, she is known to have established her reputation as a botanist during the 1750s. One of her most important contributions to botany, her description of the gardenia, was included in an Edinburgh publication titled *Essays and Observations*. Her work on plant classification was published in a Scottish scientific journal in 1770, four years after her death. After marrying Farquhar in 1759, Colden is thought to have spent her remaining years housekeeping and raising her only child, who died in 1766. Colden died the same year, on March 10, 1766.

For further research

James, Edward T., and others, eds. *Notable American Women, 1607–1950,* Volume I. Cambridge, MA: Belknap Press of Harvard University Press, 1971, pp. 357–58.

Johnson, Allen, and others, eds. *Dictionary of American Biography.* New York: Scribner, 1946–58.

Christopher Columbus

1451
Genoa, Italy
May 20, 1506
Valladolid, Spain

Italian explorer

C hristopher Columbus was the Italian explorer credited with "discovering" the New World (a European term for the continents of North America and South America). Columbus made four voyages to the Caribbean and South America between 1492 and 1504. As governor of Hispaniola (an island in the Caribbean), he oversaw the establishment of the first European settlements in the Americas. Columbus later brought over other Europeans, an act that resulted in devastating consequences to the people he called "Indians." The mistreatment of Native Americans by the Spanish colonists was so cruel that it became known in Europe as "the black legend"—a terrible story of tyranny (the abuse of power) and exploitation. Beginning with Columbus's brutal rule, the Native Americans of Hispaniola were soon virtually exterminated. Although he made great strides in Spain's effort to colonize the New World, Columbus was taken from Hispaniola in chains and under arrest, his career and reputation permanently damaged.

Seeks sponsor for expedition

Christopher Columbus was born in the city of Genoa, Italy, in 1451. His family, who made and traded woolen fab-

"Thirty-three days after my departure from Cadiz I reached the Indian sea, where I discovered many islands, thickly peopled, of which I took possession without resistance in the name of our most illustrious Monarch, . . . "

Christopher Columbus.

Portrait: Christopher Columbus. *Reproduced by permission of Corbis-Bettmann.*

59

rics, had lived in Genoa for at least three generations. From a young age, Columbus worked as a sailor on merchant and war ships in the Mediterranean Sea. In 1476 he went to Lisbon, Portugal, where he learned mathematics and astronomy (study of the stars), subjects that are vital for navigation. He made several voyages, including one to Iceland (an island between the North Atlantic and Arctic Oceans). In 1478 he married and settled on Madeira (an island off the northwest coast of Africa), where his son Diego was born. In 1488 he had another son, Fernando, with his Spanish mistress, Beatriz Enriquez.

In the early 1480s Columbus began to seek a sponsor for an expedition to Asia. He wanted to prove his theory that it would be faster and easier to get to Asia by sailing west across the Atlantic Ocean instead of going around Africa and into the Indian Ocean. For several years Columbus proposed his idea to the king of Portugal, but he was turned down. Not to be discouraged, Columbus went to try his luck in Spain. He first met with Queen Isabella I in 1486. Finally, in April 1492, Isabella and her husband, King Ferdinand V, signed an agreement with Columbus in which they agreed to pay for his voyage. According to this deal, Columbus would be named admiral, become the governor of any lands he discovered, and receive a tax-free ten percent share of any riches found in the new lands.

First lands in Bahamas

So it was that three ships—the *Santa Maria* (with Columbus as captain), and the *Niña* and the *Pinta*—set sail on an historic journey on August 3, 1492. The ships made good progress across the Atlantic, but as the weeks passed the crew wondered if they would ever reach land. According to Columbus's calculations, they already should have reached their destination. By October 10, the men began to turn mutinous (rebellious), demanding that the ships turn back toward Spain. But the next day some sailors saw signs of land: branches with green leaves and flowers floating in the water. Early the following morning a lookout (a sailor who keeps watch atop a ship mast) on the *Pinta* sighted white cliffs in the moonlight and shouted, *"Tierra! Tierra!"* ("Land! Land!").

They had found a small island in the present-day Bahamas (a group of islands southeast of Florida). Not know-

ing where they were, Columbus incorrectly assumed he had reached Asia, or the "Indies." He therefore gave the name "Indians" to the Tainos (Native Americans who inhabited the island) he met there. When the Tainos told Columbus about a larger island to the south, he thought it must be part of China or Japan. Actually it was the island we now call Cuba.

Founds Hispaniola

After leaving the Bahamas, Columbus spent a month sailing along the coast of Cuba in search of gold. In early December 1492 he reached another large island, which he named Hispaniola (or *Española*, the Spanish word for Spain) because it reminded him so much of Spain. (Today Hispaniola is comprised of the countries of Haiti and the Dominican Republic.) While sailing along the coast Columbus met an important Native American chief who was wearing gold ornaments that he gladly traded for European goods. On Christmas

Map of Christopher Columbus's route during his first voyage in 1492.
Reproduced by permission of The Granger Collection Ltd.

Eve, Columbus invited the chief and his people to come aboard the *Santa Maria* for a holiday celebration. When the party was over, everyone fell asleep and the *Santa Maria* hit a coral reef. The ship was damaged beyond repair.

The Native Americans helped the Spanish sailors unload most of the goods from the ship and carry them to shore. Columbus then founded the first European settlement in the Americas on that site, a small bay where the Haitian village of Limonade-Bord-de-Mer now stands. He named the settlement La Navidad ("the birth") in honor of the fact that the colony was founded on Christmas Day. When Columbus left La Navidad a few weeks later to return to Spain, twenty-one of his men remained at the settlement. Thus began the Spanish colonization of the Americas.

A new settlement at Isabela

When Columbus returned to Spain, he had no trouble winning support for a second voyage. After all, he had "discovered" previously unknown lands and had also brought evidence of gold and other riches. This time he was given seventeen ships that held more than one thousand colonists. But when they reached La Navidad in November 1493, the settlement lay in ruins, and unburied Spaniard bodies were everywhere. Either the Native Americans had turned against the Europeans, or the Spaniards had fought among themselves. No one had survived to tell the story.

Abandoning the site, Columbus took his new colonists seventy-five miles east, where he built a settlement called Isabela. He wasted no time in searching for the gold that would enrich Spain and secure his position and power. Only four days after landing at Isabela, Columbus sent one of his officers, Alonso de Ojeda, to look for gold. Ojeda found a small amount of the precious mineral in the mountains. Meanwhile, as Columbus was exploring nearby islands, a curious incident occurred. At one point Columbus gathered all his men together and made them swear that they had been sailing along the mainland of Asia, not the coast of an island. He was still convinced—or was trying to convince himself—that he had found the "Indies." If he suspected he had made a geographical error, he apparently did not want news of it to come from his men.

Spanish abuses of Native Americans

Bartolomé de Las Casas, a Spanish missionary who devoted his life to protecting the Native peoples of the New World, witnessed many horrible abuses of Native Americans on Hispaniola. He reported that Spaniards "made bets as to who would slit a man in two, or cut off his head at one blow. . . . They tore the babes from their mother's breast by their feet, and dashed their heads against the rocks. . . . They spitted [held like meat over a fire] the bodies of other babes, together with their mothers and all who were before them, on their swords." He also described the psychological impact of the mistreatment:

In this time, the greatest outrages and slaughterings of people were perpetrated,

whole villages being depopulated. . . . The Indians saw that without any offence on their part they were despoiled [robbed] of their kingdoms, their lands and liberties and of their lives, their wives, and homes. As they saw themselves each day perishing by the cruel and inhuman treatment of the Spaniards, crushed to the earth by the horses, cut in pieces by swords, eaten and torn by dogs, many buried alive and suffering all kinds of exquisite [extreme] tortures, some of the Princes . . . decided to abandon themselves to their unhappy fate with no further struggles, placing themselves in the hands of their enemies that they might do with them as they liked. There were still those people who fled to the mountains.

Source: The Conquest of Paradise: Christopher Columbus and the Columbian Legacy. *New York: Knopf, 1990.*

"Innumerable outrages"

When Columbus returned to Isabela in late September 1494, he found tensions growing between the Native Americans and the Spaniards. The colonists were severely mistreating the Native Americans—taking them as slaves, beating them, and stealing from them. By this time the Native Americans were fighting back, and they organized an army to drive the Europeans off the island. The Spanish took harsh steps to subdue the Native Americans, including an attack led by Columbus and his brother Bartholomew in March 1495. The Native Americans, who were no match for the Spanish army of 220 soldiers, were completely defeated. During the next few years the Native people of Hispaniola were rapidly driven toward extinction.

The Spaniards governed harshly in Hispaniola. Columbus instituted a tribute system, which required every Native American over the age of fourteen to deliver a certain amount of gold to the Spanish every three months. Those who did not pay the tribute would receive severe punishment such as having their hands cut off. Another formal policy of the government was forced labor. Colonists were assigned Native Americans to use as they liked for performing strenuous tasks, such as farming or mining. Native American offenses against the Spanish were punished with hanging, burning at the stake, beheading, or amputation (cutting off arms or legs). Meanwhile the Spaniards acted without restraint or humanity, often attacking or killing men, women, and children on a whim. Other Native Americans were taken to Spain to be sold as slaves—thirty by Columbus himself and later three hundred by his brother Bartholomew.

Native Americans also died because of the diseases the Europeans brought with them. The original inhabitants of Hispaniola had had no previous contact with such illnesses, and therefore they had no resistance. Deadly diseases like smallpox (a skin disorder caused by a virus) proved fatal to the Native Americans of Hispaniola, and later of South America. Meanwhile, the first unfavorable reports about conditions in Hispaniola were beginning to reach King Ferdinand and Queen Isabella in Spain.

Recalled to Spain

The Spanish monarchs were displeased because little gold was being sent to Spain, the colonists on Hispaniola had voiced complaints about Columbus's rule, and almost no Native Americans had been converted to Catholicism. Columbus returned to Spain in 1496 to explain the situation. By now Ferdinand and Isabella had lost most of their confidence in his ability to govern the colony. It was some time before he could convince them to send him back to Hispaniola. During the two years he spent trying to restore their faith in him, Columbus wore the coarse dress of a Franciscan friar (member of the Roman Catholic monastic order of Saint Francis). His strange attire has never been completely understood. Some historians speculate that he may have adopted it out of regret for wrongdoing, to show humility, or even as a disguise.

Finally the king and queen gave Columbus another chance, putting him in command of a small fleet carrying supplies to Hispaniola. He set sail in May 1498. During this third voyage he observed the coast of Venezuela, therefore becoming the first European to see the continent of South America. Columbus had left his brother Bartholomew in command at Isabela. Since Columbus's departure Bartholomew had moved the settlement to the south side of the island to a place the Spaniards named Santo Domingo. Columbus reached the new location in August 1498, and for the next two years governed the island. Soon after Columbus took over, the colonists rebelled against his authority.

Colonists rebel

The Spanish colonists had many reasons to rebel. Prior to a big gold strike in late 1499, any gold found was in small quantities and required a great deal of labor to extract. Because so many Native Americans had either run away or died, the Spaniards could not get enough workers to farm or mine for gold. There was constant conflict between the remaining Native Americans and the colonists. At any given time a large number of colonists were sick with deadly diseases. Supplies were also scarce and living conditions were poor. Life on Hispaniola was not what Spanish colonists expected. By 1498 they were openly challenging the Columbus's authority.

Indeed Columbus did seem to make a very poor governor. It appears he was more interested in managing his own fortune and promoting himself to the Spanish crown (the king and queen) than in solving the problems of the colonists. In a letter to Ferdinand and Isabella he even complained that he wanted "to escape from governing a dissolute [immoral] people [the Spanish] who fear neither God nor their king and queen, being full of folly and malice." He seems to have had little talent for leadership, at some points being harsh and tyrannical and, at others, neglectful of his duties. Columbus did not have the respect of the Spanish settlers, and he could not maintain order.

Columbus arrested

The Spanish king and queen continued to receive complaints about the Columbus brothers. Finally they sent a trusted knight, Francisco de Bobadilla, to replace Columbus as the new governor of Hispaniola. When de Bobadilla arrived in Santo Domingo in August 1500, he found the Spanish colony in chaos. The bodies of seven rebel Spaniards were hanging in the town square, and Columbus's brother Diego was planning to hang five more the following day. Columbus himself was not in Santo Domingo because he had gone to subdue a rebellion on another part of the island. His other brother, Bartholomew, was dealing with similar problems elsewhere. De Bobadilla immediately put Diego in jail, then arrested the other two brothers.

The colonists made serious accusations against Columbus and his brothers. After a hearing de Bobadilla decided to send them back to Spain for trial. In chains, the three brothers walked to the ships that would take them to Europe. Crowds of angry colonists shouted insults at them as they passed. It was a painful moment for Columbus. He later described his "great dishonor" this way to the king and queen: "Suddenly, when I was expecting the arrival of ships to take me to your royal presence, bearing triumph and great tidings of gold, in great joy and security, I was arrested and cast into a ship with my two brothers, shackled with chains and naked in body, and treated very badly, without being brought to trial or convicted." After months as a prisoner, Columbus was summoned to see the king and queen. He tried to convince them of his innocence and asked for the restoration of all his titles, including governor. They permitted him to keep the title of admiral, but they named Nicolás de Ovando the new governor of Hispaniola.

Final voyage a disaster

In 1502 Columbus set out on one more voyage of exploration to the Caribbean. This final trip was beset with misfortune and humiliation, however, and did nothing to improve his position with the king and queen. He actually had to be rescued after spending a year stranded on the island of Jamaica. Eventually he made his way back to Spain. Columbus asked to be sent to sea again, but King Ferdinand refused his request. Although he was ill, he had made a fortune during his time on Hispaniola. Retiring to a house in Valladolid, Spain, Columbus died shortly thereafter, in 1506.

For further research

Christopher Columbus and his Voyages. http://www.deil.lang.uiuc.edu/web.pages/holidays/Columbus.html Available July 13, 1999.

Columbus and the Age of Discovery. http://www.millersv.edu/_columbus/mainmenu.html Available July 13, 1999.

Columbus and the Native Americans. http://www.geocities.com/Capitol-Hill/8533/columbus.html Available July 13, 1999.

Columbus, Christopher. *The Voyage of Christopher Columbus: Columbus's Own Journal of Discovery.* John Cummins, translator. New York: St. Martin's Press, 1992.

Sale, Kirkpatrick, *The Conquest of Paradise: Christopher Columbus and the Columbian Legacy.* New York: Knopf, 1990.

Wilford, John Noble. *The Mysterious History of Columbus: An Exploration of the Man, the Myth, the Legacy.* New York: Knopf, distributed by Random House, 1991.

Yewell, John, and others, eds. *Confronting Columbus: An Anthology.* Jefferson, NC: McFarland and Co., 1992.

Francisco Vásquez de Coronado

February 25, 1510
Salamanca, Spain
September 22, 1554
Mexico City, Mexico

Spanish conquistador

> "Neither gold nor silver nor any trace of either was found."
>
> *A member of Coronado's exploration party.*

F rancisco Vásquez de Coronado was a Spanish conquistador (Spanish military leader) who was duped into believing that he could find fabulous cities filled with gold in the New World (a European term for the continents of North America and South America). In 1538, as governor of New Galicia (a province northwest of present-day Mexico City), Coronado headed an expedition to locate these cities full of gold and claim their treasures for Spain. During his three-year search for riches he explored parts of the Rio Grande River Valley and Kansas, and became the first European to reach Palo Duro Canyon (near present-day Amarillo, Texas). Yet Coronado returned empty-handed and was later accused of brutal treatment of Native Americans in his army. However, he was eventually exonerated of the charges.

Seeks "Seven Cities of Cibola"

Francisco Vásquez de Coronado was born in 1510 in Salamanca, Spain, into a family of minor nobility. He sailed to Mexico in 1535 as a member of the party of Antonio de Mendoza, the first viceroy (one who rules in the name of the king)

Coronado and the Spanish conquistadors

Francisco Vásquez de Coronado, one of the greatest explorers in history, was a Spanish conquistador. The conquistadors were Spanish military leaders who ruled the New World during the sixteenth century. The first conquistadors were Francisco Pizarro, who conquered Peru, and Hernán Cortés, who conquered Mexico. Antonio de Mendoza, who ruled Mexico and Peru, was also a conquistador.

As a viceroy (one who rules in the name of the king), Mendoza continued the conquest begun by Cortés and established the foundation for Spanish rule in the New World for years to come. Although most conquistadors were considered ruthless, Mendoza was more civilized. Known as "the good viceroy," he encouraged education and religion, improved conditions for Native Americans, and brought the first printing press to America. He also expanded exploration northward.

Álvar Núñez Cabeza de Vaca (whose name means "cow's head" in Spanish) was another well-known Spanish conquistador. He arrived in the New World in 1528. The story of his escape from Native Americans with the Moroccan slave Estevanico and two other men led to the legend of the fabulous "Seven Cities of Cibola." This tale grew after Fray Marcos de Niza wrote a fantastic version of Cabeza de Vaca's adventures. Inspired by the words of Fray Marcos, Coronado attempted but failed to discover the cities. Cabeza de Vaca eventually became governor of the Rio de la Plata region in South America.

of New Spain, as Mexico was then called. After arriving in Mexico, Coronado married Beatriz de Estrada, the wealthy heiress of the former treasurer of New Spain. He took part in crushing an uprising in the Spanish royal mines and in October 1538 was named governor of New Galicia, a province on the west coast of Mexico. As governor he had jurisdiction over Spanish explorations on the northern frontier.

Soon after taking over his duties, Coronado outfitted an expedition led by **Estevanico** (see entry), a "Moorish" (part African) slave, and Fray Marcos de Niza, a Franciscan friar (member of a Catholic religious order). They were heading north to verify reports of the fabulous "Seven Cities of Cibola" that had been brought to Mexico by Estevanico, who had been

a guide on an earlier expedition headed by Álvar Núñez Cabeza de Vaca.

Fray Marcos and Estevanico left the town of Culiacán (the present-day capital of Sinaloa, a state in Mexico) on March 7, 1539. He returned alone about five and a half months later, since Estevanico had been killed at the pueblo (Native American communal dwelling) of Hawikuh. Fray Marcos said he had seen the very rich and very large city of Cibola from a distance. It is believed that he was referring to Hawikuh, which in actuality is a small pueblo. Since his own journal was contradictory, Fray Marcos embellished the story and ignited what would be an ill-fated expedition. At the time, however, Coronado was impressed enough to make plans to travel with Fray Marcos to Mexico City and bring back a report to Mendoza.

Discovers deception

Mendoza had long been interested in exploring the territory north of Mexico and was convinced by the friar's sto-

Francisco Vásquez de Coronado and his force during their journey through what is now New Mexico. *Reproduced by permission of The Library of Congress.*

ries that further exploration might bring him wealth and power. He decided to equip an expedition at royal expense and named Coronado to head the venture. Coronado assembled a force of about three hundred Spaniards and nearly a thousand Native Americans at the west coast town of Compostela. Mendoza traveled to Compostela to review the expedition in person before it started out on February 25, 1540. The viceroy also sent two ships up the Gulf of California under the command of Hernando de Alarcón to support the expedition from the sea. Losing contact with Coronado, the ships sailed two hundred miles up the Colorado River.

Coronado traveled with his army to Culiacán. On April 22, he left with an advance force of about one hundred Spaniards, a number of Native Americans, and four friars. They proceeded up the Yaqui River valley (in present-day New Mexico), where they founded the town of San Geronimo. Leaving one of his officers, Melchor Díaz, in charge, Coronado took a group of soldiers toward the Gila River (in present-day New

Mexico and Arizona). Díaz went up the Colorado near present-day Yuma, Arizona, and crossed into territory that is now California. He became the first European to explore this region. Meanwhile, Coronado and his men had crossed the Gila River and entered the Colorado Plateau. They reached Hawikuh in what is now western New Mexico in early July. The Spanish had no difficulty in capturing the town, but once inside they realized it did not come close to matching Fray Marcos's glowing description of wealth and riches. As a result, Coronado sent the friar back to Mexico in disgrace. One observer reported, "such were the curses that some hurled at Fray Marcos that I pray God may protect him from them."

On July 15 Coronado sent Pedro de Tovar and Fray Juan Padilla northwest to a province called Tusayan. They encountered the ancient villages of the Hopi (a Native American tribe) in what is now northern Arizona. Then they heard about a great river—the Colorado—to the west. The following month Garcia López de Cárdenas led a group in search of the river. Finally, they reached the edge of a great canyon and became the first Europeans to see Grand Canyon, one of the world's natural wonders.

The "Tiguex War"

In late August 1540 Coronado sent out another party to the east under the command of Pedro de Alvarado. They reached the pueblo of Acoma, perched high on a rock, where the inhabitants gave the Spaniards food. Alvarado then went to the town of Tiguex in the Rio Grande valley (near present-day Bemalillo). When he reported back that Tiguex had plenty of food supplies, Coronado decided to make his headquarters there. During the winter of 1540–41 the demands of the Spaniards for supplies, as well as conflict over women, led to the "Tiguex War." After capturing one pueblo, the Spanish burned two hundred of their captives alive. Several Spaniards were also killed during various engagements, and Coronado was wounded many times.

Coronado foiled again

Alvarado then traveled to the east to Cicuye (on the Pecos River), where he captured a Plains Indian (perhaps a

Pawnee), whom the Spanish named "the Turk." The Turk told stories of the land of Quivira that was ruled by a powerful king and contained abundant quantities of gold. On April 23, 1541, Coronado left Tiguex to find Quivira and headed eastward into the Great Plains, where the Spanish saw enormous herds of buffalo. When they finally observed the meager material possessions of the nomadic Plains tribes, the Spanish realized they had been duped once again. A frustrated Coronado sent his main force back to the Rio Grand with large supplies of buffalo meat. He then took command of a small detachment that headed north and east for forty-two days, probably reaching central Kansas near the present-day town of Lyons. A member of the party reported that "Neither gold nor silver nor any trace of either was found." When the Turk confessed that he had lied in order to draw the Spaniards into the interior, some of the soldiers strangled him to death. (It is said that Coronado opposed his execution.)

The People

The story of Coronado is told in *The People* (1996), a Public Broadcasting System (PBS) television documentary on exploration and discovery in the American West. The program is available on videocassette.

Coronado charged with brutality

Now completely defeated, Coronado returned to Tiguex in October 1541. Shortly thereafter he was seriously injured in a riding accident and lingered near death for some time. By early 1542 the Spaniards were ready to return to Mexico. They left Tiguex in April and arrived in Mexico City in late autumn. Mendoza was angry that the expedition had not resulted in the discovery of treasures, but he gradually realized that Coronado had done his best. Mendoza reappointed Coronado governor of New Galicia in 1544.

In May 1544, however, a royal judge began a formal investigation of accusations that Coronado was guilty of brutality to the Native Americans. He was relieved of his duties as governor but was cleared of all charges two years later. He then became an official in the municipal government of Mexico City. In 1547 Coronado testified in favor of Mendoza during an investigation of the viceroy's rule. In reward for his services, he was given a land grant in 1549. Coronado's health continued to decline, however, and he died in Mexico City on September 22, 1554.

For further research

Bolton, Herbert E. *Coronado: Knight of the Pueblos and Plains*. Albuquerque: University of New Mexico Press, 1964.

"Francisco Vásquez de Coronado." http://www.win.tue.nl/cs/fm/engels/discovery/coronado.html Available July 13, 1999.

Jacobs, William Jay. *Coronado: Dreamer in Golden Armor*. New York: F. Watts, 1994.

The People. Public Broadcasting System, 1996. Videocassette recording.

Syme, Ronald. *Francisco Coronado and the Seven Cities of Gold*. New York: Morrow, 1965.

John Cotton

December 4, 1584
Derby, Derbyshire, England
December 23, 1652
Boston, Massachusetts

Puritan clergyman

John Cotton was a prominent clergyman in the Massachusetts Bay Colony during the seventeenth century. After introducing Puritanism (a religious philosophy that stresses strict moral and spiritual codes) to a church in England, he emigrated (moved from one country to another) to the New World (the European term for North America and South America) and continued his religious activities. He arrived in Massachusetts in 1633 and quickly became an influential leader of the colony. As a preacher he was interested in both religion and politics, arguing against those who believed the two should remain separate. He participated in many of the major political and religious conflicts that took place in the colony, including the trial of religious heretic (one who violates the laws of the church) **Anne Hutchinson** (see entry).

Becomes a preacher in England

John Cotton was born at Derby, Derbyshire, England, on December 4, 1584, to devoutly Christian parents. His father, Roland Cotton, was a wealthy lawyer. Little is known about Cotton's childhood, except that he attended Derby

"Democracy I do not conceyve that ever God did ordene as a fitt government eyther for church or commonwealth."

John Cotton.

Cotton's preaching inspires revolution

In addition to altering the liturgy of the Church of England (the official religion of England, also known as the Anglican Church), John Cotton sought to change Puritan doctrine. He focused mainly on the belief that good works earn salvation, known as the Covenant of Works. In a radical move, Cotton claimed that it was possible to obtain salvation through direct revelation from God. Therefore, he advanced what was known as the Covenant of Grace. This turned out to be a popular doctrine because it freed believers from having to do good works to earn salvation. Instead, they could claim that God had given them the means for eternal salvation. Cotton urged his followers to adhere to the doctrine of good works whether or not they had received divine revelation from God.

After emigrating to Boston in the Massachusetts Bay Colony in 1633, Cotton continued preaching the Covenant of Grace. One of his most enthusiastic followers was Anne Hutchinson, who believed strongly in the doctrine. She even began to hold private meetings in Boston, during which she advanced her own extreme version of Cotton's teachings. Hutchinson believed that individuals who had received direct revelation from God were completely free from having to do good works. The Covenant of Grace now bordered upon Antimonian heresy, which freed Christians from the moral law of the Old Testament. It was still a popular doctrine, however, and Hutchinson had a massive following that threatened the very foundation of Puritan society in Massachusetts.

Grammar School from 1593 to 1597. As a young man Cotton showed a natural ability for scholarship. In 1597, when he was only thirteen, Cotton began attending Trinity College at Cambridge University. He received a bachelor of arts degree in 1603, and a master of arts degree in 1606.

After mastering Hebrew, Cotton was awarded a fellowship to Emmanuel College at Cambridge University in 1603. Founded by a Puritan, Emmanuel College was the most Puritan of any college in the Cambridge system. At Emmanuel, Cotton served as a dean and head lecturer, and became an influential preacher at St. Mary's Church. During the six years he spent at Emmanuel College, he claimed to have experienced a religious conversion to Puritanism after witnessing the preaching of Richard Sibbes. On July 13, 1610, Cotton became a priest in Lincoln, England, and in 1613 he received a bachelor of divinity degree. In July of the same year, Cotton married Elizabeth Horrocks.

Alters liturgy to favor Puritanism

On June 24, 1612, Cotton was elected vicar (a Church of England official) of St. Botolph's Church in Boston, a port city in Lincolnshire. Although he was only twenty-seven at the time, he had already gained a reputation as an inspiring preacher. Around 1615 Cotton began to alter the liturgy (the accepted way to worship) of the church toward Puritanism. He did this by abandoning certain ceremonies and practices of the Church of England, in favor of the simpler Puritan ways. Cotton was respected by many of the parishioners at St. Botolph's, but only a few accepted his conversion to Puritanism. He was eventually replaced by an assistant who followed the traditions of the Church of England. Meanwhile, Cotton was permitted to continue preaching Puritanism at St. Botolph's.

Although some church authorities protested, no action was ever taken against Cotton for his nonconformity. He spent a total of twenty years at St. Botolph's, and throughout most of this time he preached Puritanism. Cotton received considerable leniency from the bishop and apparently gained further protection from King James I. Even when a group of Puritans vandalized the church in 1621 by breaking stained glass windows and defacing monuments, Cotton was not accused in connection with the incident. After being summoned to appear before the Court of High Commission in 1632, however, he fled to London. Finally, on May 7, 1633, he resigned as vicar of St. Botolph's Church.

Becomes prominent figure

After Elizabeth Cotton died in 1630, Cotton married Sarah (Hawkridge) Story two years later. He then set his sights on emigrating to the Massachusetts Bay Colony. He had become interested in the colony when he delivered a sermon in 1630 to a group of Puritans that included **John Winthrop** (see entry), who were going to Massachusetts. In July 1633 the Cottons left England for the New World on board the *Griffin*. On

Excerpt from "God's Promise to His Plantations" (1630)

Before moving from England to the Massachusetts Bay Colony in 1633, John Cotton wrote "God's Promise to His Plantations." Drawing from passages in the Bible, he compared doing God's work to planting a garden. Cotton's metaphor appealed to his fellow Puritans, who used it to describe their mission in starting colonies in North America. Following is an excerpt from the work:

Quest[ion]. What is it for God to plant a people?

Answ[e]r. It is a Metaphor taken from young Impes; I will plant them, that is, I will make them to take roote there; and that is, where they and their soyle agree well together, when they are well and sufficiently provided for, as a plant suckes nourishment from the soyle that fitteth it.

Secondly, When hee causeth them to grow as plants doe, in Psal. [Psalms] 80. 8, 9, 10, 11. When a man growes like a tree in tallnesse and strength, to more firmnesse and eminency (prominence), then hee may be said to be planted.

Thirdly, When God causeth them to fructifie [bear fruit]. Psal. 1.5.

Fourthly, When he establisheth them there, then he plants, and rootes not up.

But here is something more especiall in this planting; for they were planted before in this land, and yet he promiseth here againe, that he will plant them in their owne land; which doth imply first, That whatever former good estate they had already, he would prosper it, and increase it. . . .

Source: Gunn, Giles. Early American Writing. *New York: Penguin Books, 1994, pp. 102–03.*

---

the voyage Sarah gave birth to their first son, whom they named Seaborn. Other prominent members of the group included John Haynes, Edmund Quincy, and Thomas Hooker. The *Griffin* anchored at Boston, Massachusetts, on September 4.

Interested in both politics and religion, Cotton quickly became a prominent figure in the Massachusetts Bay Colony. As a leader, he was involved in most of the controversial issues and major conflicts that took place at the time. For instance, when the Antimonian controversy disrupted the colony, Cotton participated in Hutchinson's prosecution for heresy. (Antimonianism stated that Christians were free from the moral obligations of the Old Testament, the first part of the Bible. This view was considered heresy, or violation of Puritan church laws, which relied on the Bible as the source of the

Word of God.) At first he was on Hutchinson's side. However, after realizing that she had no other supporters, Cotton joined the prosecution. Hutchinson was excommunicated (excluded from the rights of the church) and banished from the colony in 1638. Cotton was also involved in two disputes with **Roger Williams** (see entry). In the first, he disagreed with Williams's belief that all Puritans must officially renounce (refuse) the Church of England. In the second, Williams asserted that colonial magistrates (officials entrusted with the administration of laws) should have no power over the religious choices of individuals. Believing that it was impossible to separate religion and politics, Cotton argued that magistrates should have secular (not specifically religious) as well as religious authority. This power would give magistrates absolute power over their citizens.

Cotton was an industrious colonial leader, and was known for his tireless energy. He felt that a serious scholar should work twelve-hour days, and he conducted church services that lasted six hours. In addition to his preaching duties, he wrote many books on the methods and theories of Puritanism. One important work was *The Keys of the Kingdom of Heaven* (1644). Probably the most widely read of his books was *The Way of the Churches of Christ in New England* (1645). He defended his books against critics with *The Way of the Congregational Churches Cleared* (1648). Cotton's catechism (religious instruction book), *Spiritual Milk for Boston Babes in Either England* (1645), became a popular manual for bringing up children in New England. Considered one of the best defenders of Puritanism, Cotton was invited to England in 1643 to attend the Westminster Assembly. He decided not to go. After becoming

Spiritual·
MILK
FOR
BOSTON BABES
In either ENGLAND.

Drawn out of the Breasts of both *TEST AMENTS* for their souls nourishment

But may be of like use to any Children

By JOHN COTTON, *B. D.*
late Teacher to the Church of Boston in New-England.

C A M B R I D G
Printed by S. G. for Hezekiah Usher at Boston in New-England
1 6 5 6

Title page from John Cotton's catechism, *Spiritual Milk for Boston Babes in Either England.* *Reproduced by permission of The Granger Collection Ltd.*

the Congregational leader in New England in 1646, he was chosen to create a new model for church government, but his plan was not accepted.

Transformed by conservativism

Historians are certain that Cotton was one of the finest colonial leaders of his day. They also note, however, that much of his potential was limited by the narrowly conservative environment in Massachusetts. For instance, Cotton began his career by defying the Church of England, but in the New World he became a conformist (one who adhered to the teachings of the Church of England). Eventually he formed the belief that colonial magistrates should have absolute power over citizens and, further, that magistrates should be allowed to use executions to preserve order. In addition, Cotton rejected democracy and the power of the common man. He agreed with other colonial leaders such as Winthrop, who contended that government should be run by a small, elite group. Cotton remained active in both politics and religion until the end of his life. In late 1652 he caught a cold while preaching to students at Harvard College in Cambridge, Massachusetts. Developing serious respiratory problems, he gave his last sermon on November 21, 1652. He died a month later in Boston.

For further research

Gunn, Giles. *Early American Writing*. New York: Penguin Books, 1994, pp. 102–03.

Johnson, Allen, and others, eds. *Dictionary of American Biography.* New York: Scribner, 1946–1958, pp. 460–62.

Ziff, Larzer. *The Career of John Cotton: Puritanism and the American Experience.* Princeton, New Jersey: Princeton University Press, 1962.

George Croghan

1720
near Dublin, Ireland
1782
Philadelphia, Pennsylvania

Trader, Indian agent, and landowner

George Croghan was a trader and landowner in the English colony of Pennsylvania during the expansion of the western frontier. In Croghan's day, the frontier was the boundary between Pennsylvania and the unsettled territory that became Ohio. An adventurous man, Croghan was enthusiastic about trading with the Native Americans in that region, and he established friendly relations with the Seneca tribe around Lake Erie. The French were dominant in this region and soon came into conflict with the English, whom Croghan represented. Croghan's attempts to bolster trade in the Pennsylvania colony became legendary.

Becomes trader

George Croghan was born in Ireland. He left Ireland in 1741 during a potato famine (failure of potato crops that resulted in widespread starvation) and settled in the Pennsylvania colony. At the time he arrived, trade between colonists and Native Americans had expanded westward beyond the Allegheny Mountains and into Ohio. Commerce was now thriving along the banks of the Ohio River and the shores of

"I always took him for an honest man, and have as yet no reason to think otherwys [sic] of him."

Conrad Weiser, U.S. Indian Affairs Advisor.

Portrait: George Croghan.
Reproduced by permission of Archive Photos, Inc.

81

Lake Erie. Wealthy Pennsylvania merchants like Edward Shippen made a lot of money exchanging European goods for Native American furs (at the time such transactions were called "the Indian trade"). The first historical reference to Croghan is dated June 1742, when he was asked to deliver some goods from Shippen to Peter Tostee, another prominent Pennsylvania trader who had brought Croghan into the trading business. Several months later Croghan accompanied Tostee on a venture in Ohio.

In 1743 Croghan purchased land in Lancaster, Pennsylvania. The following year he launched an expedition to trade with the Senecas, whose village was located near the mouth of the Cuyahoga River on Lake Erie (the area that is now Cleveland, Ohio). The Lake Erie region had already been claimed by the French, whose headquarters were in Detroit (in present-day Michigan). At the time, French traders were attempting to gain control of the region by urging allied Native American tribes to attack the English. In March 1744, England declared war on France. During the following winter Croghan remained at the Seneca village and continued trading. In the spring of 1745, however, he had to flee after a Frenchman accused him of trespassing.

On his way to Philadelphia, Pennsylvania, Croghan met up with Tostee's trading party. Tostee reported that he and his men had just been attacked by Shawnee Indians who were allied with the French. During the conflict, the Shawnee had taken everything, including some furs that belonged to Croghan. When the Croghan and Trostee parties reached Philadelphia they met with Shippen, who was now mayor of the city. In an attempt to influence any remaining Shawnee who were not allied with the French, the Pennsylvania Council (the governing body of the colony) decided to offer a gift of European-made goods to the Native Americans. This plan, which was not traditional government practice, was probably Croghan's idea. He would continue to use this method to convince Ohio tribes not to join the French.

Builds plantation and becomes important trader

In 1746 Croghan purchased 171 acres of land on the Conedogwinet Creek in Pennsborough Township. On the land he built Pennsborough plantation, which would be his home for the next five years. The following winter he returned to Ohio to live among the Senecas at Cuyahoga in the Lake Erie region. Meanwhile, the English gained dominance in the area and Croghan conducted more trade than ever before. In response to the strong English presence, the French commander at Detroit was ordered to send Native Americans to attack the English traders. This effort failed, however, because many Native Americans were ending their alliances with the French.

By now Pennsborough plantation had become Croghan's headquarters for trade with Native peoples in Ohio. Furs and other Native American goods were shipped from the plantation in the same wagons that had delivered European products. On the estate he operated a tannery (a shop where animal hides are made into leather) and a shop where Native American goods were sold to the public. He also raised cattle and horses and owned African slaves.

Attack sparks uprising

An important center of trade in the Lake Erie region was the village of Sandusky (now a city in Ohio). Croghan's growing business interests played a big part in the success of Sandusky. In 1747, the village was also the site of a massacre that sparked a major uprising. Five French traders on their way to Detroit stopped in Sandusky, not knowing that local Native Americans were loyal to the English. They were attacked and murdered by Wyandots and Senecas. Afterwards, Native groups mounted raids in the entire area, searching for other French traders who had ventured into English territory. Although the French were ultimately victorious, they lost many men and one of their forts was partially burned. The French directly blamed Croghan and the English for sparking the Native American attacks.

During the uprising the Pennsylvania Council made another gift of European goods to the Ohio tribes to ensure their continued support against the French. Once again the plan was Croghan's idea. The chief governmental adviser on Indian affairs, Conrad Weiser, agreed to Croghan's suggestion that the Native Americans be given a huge shipment of goods—including lead, gunpowder, and liquor. Accumulating these items was a major undertaking, however, and Croghan soon became concerned that the Native Americans would ally themselves with

Prosperity threatens Six Nations

The meeting between the Twightwees, a Native American tribe in present-day Ohio, and the Pennsylvania Council in 1747 was an unprecedented event. **William Penn** (see entry), the proprietor of the Pennsylvania colony, had previously dealt only with the Iroquois Confederacy. In the seventeenth century, the Iroquois Confederacy was known as the League of Five Nations, an alliance comprised of the Senecas, Cayugas, Onondagas, Oneidas, and Mohawks, Native American groups who lived in New York State. In the following century it became the League of Six Nations with the incorporation of the Tuscaroras. The Onondaga village served as the capital, where the confederacy made decisions concerning wars and treaties. However, in the 1740s, the vast contingent of Native American groups settling in Ohio threatened the power of the Six Nations. Ohio was located far from New York, and Ohio tribes were thriving because of the prosperous fur trade. As a result, tribes such as the Twightwees were able to strike out independently and make their own treaties.

the French before he could get the entire shipment together. To remedy the situation, the Pennsylvania Council decided to have him give the Native Americans a portion of the shipment.

A group of fifteen tribal representative arrived in Lancaster the day the delivery took place. Pennsylvania officials thanked the Native Americans for taking part in the uprising against the French and told the representatives that Croghan would deliver their partial gift. Weiser escorted the Native Americans to Harris's Ferry where they met with Croghan, who handed over a portion of the lead, gunpowder, and liquor. He also provided them with horses for their return trip to Ohio. Before departing, the Indians mentioned that if they had not received assistance they would have joined the French, who were gaining strength in Ohio. Croghan's quick thinking appeased the Native Americans and resulted in more English trade in Ohio.

Twightwees become English allies

Finally, in the winter of 1747, the larger gift that was promised to the Ohio Indians was ready. In addition to gunpowder and lead, this delivery also included guns, knives, and hatchets. Once again, delivery of the gift was delayed. Weiser, who was supposed to transport the shipment to Ohio, received news that the uprising had ended. Therefore, he thought the gift was unnecessary. The Pennsylvania Council, however, insisted that it be delivered whether or not the Indians were still at war. At the time, Croghan was at his Pennsborough plantation impatiently awaiting the shipment, and the council told him to proceed to Ohio to deliver a token gift and inform the Native Americans of the delay.

Croghan set out for Ohio in April. After arriving later that month, he met with Indians in Logstown, a trading post on the Ohio River. Croghan realized that he did not bring enough supplies to distribute among the one thousand five hundred Indians. Therefore, he added some of his own supplies to the token gift. At the time, in typical Croghan fashion, he had planned to charge the government for the extra supplies. During a meeting at Logstown, Native Americans informed Croghan that the Twightwee tribe had agreed to form an alliance with the English. Finally, Croghan returned to Philadelphia in June with the good news, as well as a bill for the extra supplies.

Tribes finally rewarded

Croghan informed the Pennsylvania Council that the Twightwees were to arrive at Lancaster on July 15 to negotiate a treaty. The meeting took place at the courthouse in Lancaster. Croghan, who attended the proceedings as a witness, signed his name to the treaty between the English and the Twightwees. The alliance would be highly beneficial to the English. Not only would it increase their military strength, but it would also help their trade business. Since the Twightwees controlled a vast region in Ohio and were no longer under French command, the English were now free to increase their trade activity in the area.

After the treaty was signed, Croghan set out with the Twightwees for his Pennsborough plantation. Upon returning to his plantation, Croghan began preparing the gift that he and Weiser were to deliver to Ohio. When Weiser arrived, the two men embarked on the long journey to Logstown to meet with the Native Americans, who were anxiously awaiting their arrival. The gift from the Pennsylvania Council, which had taken so long to prepare, finally reached Logstown. Weiser, acting as interpreter, informed the Native Americans that the Twightwees were now allies of the English and that the war between England and France was over.

Serves as diplomat

In 1756 Croghan began a twenty-year career as a government Indian agent for Pennsylvania. Because of his good

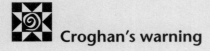

Croghan's warning

After working for many years as a successful trader, George Croghan had a twenty-year career as an agent for the Indian Department in Pennsylvania. When he was a trader he started the practice of giving gifts of such items as gunpowder, lead, and liquor to Native American tribes to win their allegiance. Although gift-giving was against English government policy, Croghan continued the practice when he worked with the Indian Department. In 1763 he wrote a letter to William Johnson, head of the department, warning of the dire consequences of not giving presents to Native Americans:

> The Indians are a very jealous people and they had great expectations of being very generally supplied by us, and from their poverty and mercenary disposition, they can't bear such a disappointment. Undoubtedly the General [Jeffrey Amherst, the British military commander in Pennsylvania] has his own reason for not allowing any presents or ammunition to be given to them, and I wish it may have its desired effect, but I take this opportunity to acquaint you that I dread the event, as I know the Indians can't long persevere. They are a rash, inconsistent people and inclined to mischief and never will consider consequences, though it may end in their ruin. Their success at the beginning of this war [the French and Indian Wars] on our frontiers is too recent in their memory to suffer them to consider their present inability to make war with us, and if the Senecas, Delawares, and Shawnees should break with us, it will end in a general war with all the western nations, though they at present seem jealous of each other. For my part, I am resolved to resign if the General does not liberalize our expenditures for Indian affairs. I don't choose to be begging eternally for such necessaries as are wanted to carry on the service, nor will I support it at my own expense. There are great troubles ahead. How it may end the Lord knows, but I assure you I am of opinion it will not be long before we shall have some quarrels with them.

Source: Eckert, Allan W. The Conquerors: A Narrative. Boston: Little, Brown, 1970, pp. 130–31.

relations with Native Americans, he was an excellent diplomat. In 1763, however, Croghan's home was burned to the ground by a Delaware raiding party. Croghan died in Philadelphia in 1782. He now stands as one of the legendary figures on the colonial frontier, and his life is regarded as a typically American success story. Along the way, he managed to forge close bonds with Native Americans and his influence was acknowledged by the government of Pennsylvania. Although his policy of rewarding the Indians with gifts was not traditional practice in Pennsylvania, it was an effective means of winning the allegiance of Ohio tribes. His success in business, as is evidenced by his thriving Pennsborough plantation operation, helped to open up the western territory for trade and eventual exploration.

For further research

Eckert, Allan W. *The Conquerors: A Narrative.* Boston: Little, Brown, 1970.

Wainwright, Nicholas B. *George Croghan: Wilderness Diplomat.* Chapel Hill: The University of North Carolina Press, 1959.

Mary Dyer

Unknown
England
June 1, 1660
Boston, Massachusetts

Quaker martyr

"In obedience to the will of the Lord God I came, and in His will I abide faithful to the death."

Mary Dyer.

Portrait: Mary Dyer.
Reproduced by permission of The Granger Collection Ltd.

Mary Dyer was an English Puritan (one who practices or preaches a strict moral and spiritual code) who emigrated to the Massachusetts Bay Colony from England in 1634 or 1635. She became influenced by **Anne Hutchinson** (see entry), who was preaching "Antimonian" ideas. (Antinomianism is the belief that faith alone is sufficient for salvation from sin. The view was considered heresy because it was contrary to the Puritan teaching that salvation can be gained only by doing good works.) When Hutchinson was excommunicated (excluded from the rights of the church) and banished from Massachusetts in 1638, Dyer also left the colony. After traveling to England with her husband in 1652, Dyer became a Quaker (member of the Religious Society of Friends who believe that the individual can receive divine truth from the Holy Spirit through his or her own "inner light" without the guidance of a minister or priest). When she returned to New England five years later she was imprisoned for her belief. Eventually, she was executed for heresy. Today Dyer is considered a symbol of religious freedom.

Marries Puritan

Mary Dyer was born Mary Barrett in England. The date of her birth is unknown, and very little information exists about her early life. Although the story is not based on fact, there is a rumor that she was the daughter of Lady Arabella Stuart, who was a cousin of King James I of England. There is some evidence, however, that she came from a wealthy family. It is also known that on October 27, 1633, she married William Dyer, a milliner (hat maker) and a Puritan. They were wed at St. Martin's-in-the-Fields, a church in London. Not long after their marriage, the Dyers, like many other Puritans, emigrated to the New World (a European term for North America and South America).

Influenced by Anne Hutchinson

The Dyers arrived at the Massachusetts Bay Colony in 1634 (or 1635) and joined the Puritan church on December 13, 1635. The Dyers were influenced by Anne Hutchinson, who preached about "Antimonianism." Unlike the Puritans, Hutchinson believed the religious experience was personal, asserting that only the individual alone could decide whether or not he or she was saved (had gained forgiveness for sins against God). The Puritans, on the other hand, turned outward for their religious experience and achieved salvation through hard work, charitable acts, and material gain. For the Puritans, church leaders had the sole authority to decide who was saved.

Because Hutchinson challenged one of the central doctrines (laws) of the Puritanism, she was excommunicated and banished from the Massachusetts Bay Colony on March 22, 1638. By this time, the Dyers were so influenced by Hutchinson that they took her side against their pastor, John Wilson. When Hutchinson left the church the day she was excommunicated, Mary Dyer followed her. As a result, the Dyers were also excommunicated. The couple settled at Newport, Rhode Island, where they could practice their form of religion freely. William Dyer went into public office and became an upstanding member of the colony. Mary Dyer turned her attention to domestic life. The couple eventually had five sons: Samuel, William, Mahershallalhashbaz, Henry, and Charles.

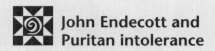

John Endecott and Puritan intolerance

The man responsible for the execution of Mary Dyer was John Endecott, the governor of the Massachusetts Bay Colony. Endecott was a strict Puritan who had emigrated to the New World in 1628. He himself had experienced religious persecution in England when he was rebuked by his grandfather, who disagreed with his views. Despite his own experience, however, Endecott gained a reputation as a strong-willed, unfeeling man. Endecott played a major role in the Pequot War of 1636, which led to the near extinction of the Pequot tribe. He was equally harsh with dissenters (religious nonconformists) and other rebels—especially Quakers—in the Massachusetts Bay Colony. After executing William Robinson and Marmaduke Stephenson the previous year, he executed Dyer in 1660. Some historians believe that Endecott was too brutal in his handling of the Quakers. However, others point to the prevailing opinion among colonists that dissenters should be executed.

Joins Society of Friends

In 1652 the Dyers returned to England on a political mission to uphold the interests of the colony with John Clarke and **Roger Williams** (see entry), founder of Rhode Island. Remaining in England for five years, Mary Dyer joined the Religious Society of Friends, the Quaker religion founded by George Fox. Quaker beliefs were very similar to Hutchinson's "Antimonianism." According to the Quaker doctrine of "inner light," each individual possessed the Holy Spirit. Like Hutchinson, the Quakers believe that the individual has a direct relationship to God. In 1657 Dyer and her husband returned to New England, settling in New Haven (now a city in Connecticut). Because of her conversion to Quaker beliefs, Dyer was immediately seized by the Puritans and imprisoned in Boston. During the previous year Puritan leaders in Boston had outlawed "the cursed sect of heretics . . . commonly called Quakers."

Dyer was released from jail when her husband promised that he would prevent her from preaching. Nevertheless, Dyer continued to advocate Quakerism and was thus expelled from New Haven. In the meantime, on October 19, 1658, the Massachusetts courts passed an even stronger law that imposed the death penalty on practicing Quakers. By the following year, two Quakers, Marmaduke Stephenson and William Robinson, were imprisoned in Boston. Defying the laws, Dyer visited the two prisoners that summer. She was subsequently thrown into prison as well. On September 12, all three of the prisoners were banished from Boston and threatened with execution if they ever returned.

Continues to defy laws

Not surprisingly, considering her rebellious spirit, Dyer returned to Boston with Stephenson, Robinson, and several other Quakers. The group was determined to confront the rigid Massachusetts laws about religious tolerance. By October 19, 1659, they were brought before the General Court to be investigated and sentenced. When asked why they had returned to Boston, they replied that "the ground and cause of their coming was of the Lord." All three Quakers were sentenced to death by Massachusetts governor **John Endecott** (see entry). On October 27, 1659, Stephenson and Robinson were hanged, but Dyer once again escaped execution. At the last minute, John Winthrop Jr. and Thomas Temple intervened with a plea from her son William. Dyer was spared from the gallows.

Becomes symbol of religious freedom

Dyer left Boston for Rhode Island and then went to Long Island (in present-day New York). She was determined to

Mary Dyer walking hand in hand with condemned Quakers William Robinson and Marmaduke Stevenson to the gallows in 1659.
Reproduced by permission of The Granger Collection Ltd.

The execution of Mary Dyer

An eyewitness and fellow Quaker gave a detailed description of the execution of Mary Dyer on May 31, 1660. Following are excerpts from that account.

So she [Dyer] was brought to the prison-house, where she was before, close shut up until the next day. . . . Then they [the Puritan authorities] brought her forth, and drums were beat before and behind her, with a band of soldiers, through the town, and so to the place of execution, which is about a mile, the drums being that none might hear her speak all the way.

Some said unto her, that if she would return she might come down and save her life. She answered and said, "Nay, I cannot. For in obedience to the will of the Lord God I came, and in his will I abide faithful to the death. . . . "

John Wilson, their [the Dyers'] priest of Boston, said, "M. Dyer, O repent; O repent, and be not so deluded and carried away by the deceit of the Devil." M. Dyer answered and said, "No, man, I am not now to repent. . . . "

Then one said she should say she had been in Paradise. And she answered, "Yea, I have been in Paradise several days." And more she spake of her eternal happiness, that's out of mind. And so sweetly and cheerfully in the Lord she finished her testimony and died a faithful martyr of Jesus Christ. . . .

. . . These are the people that say their churches are the purest churches in the world, and their magistrates are godly magistrates, and godly ministers. A fair show to the world! . . .

Reprinted in: Kupperman, Karen Ordahl, ed. Major Problems in American Colonial History. Lexington, MA: D. C. Heath and Company, 1993, pp. 162–64.

return to Boston to "desire the repeal of that wicked law against God's people and offer up her life there." On her return to Boston, she was arrested again. This time she was sentenced to death, and the penalty was carried out on May 31, 1660. Her husband, who never became a Quaker, claimed that his wife was mad and should be spared. Despite his plea, Dyer was executed. She was given one last chance to repent before she was hanged. Dyer refused to renounce her Quaker beliefs, saying, "In obedience to the will of the Lord God I came, and in His will I abide faithful to the death."

By the twentieth century—four hundred years after her execution—Dyer had become a symbol of courage in the face of tyranny (oppressive power exerted by a government). At the time she was sentenced to death, she was considered a heretic (one who does not conform to an accepted belief or doctrine). Over the years, however, freedom of religion is recognized as a central tenet (a principle or doctrine) of American law. Once seen as a threat to society, Dyer is now regarded as a hero. In 1959 the General Court of Massachusetts erected a statue in her memory on the State House grounds in Boston.

For further research

Bacon, Margaret Hope. *Mothers of Feminism.* New York: HarperCollins, 1986.

Crawford, Deborah. *Four Women in a Violent Time: Anne Hutchinson (1591–1643), Mary Dyer (1591?–1660), Lady Deborah Moody (1600–1659), Penelope Stout (1622–1732).* New York: Crown Publishers, 1970.

Kupperman, Karen Ordahl, ed. *Major Problems in American Colonial History.* Lexington, MA: D. C. Heath and Company, 1993, pp. 162–64.

Jonathan Edwards

October 5, 1703
Windsor, Connecticut
March 22, 1758
Stockbridge, Massachusetts

Puritan minister, leader of the Great Awakening

"Therefore, let every one that is out of Christ, now awake and fly from the wrath to come."

From Jonathan Edward's "Sinners in the Hands of an Angry God."

Portrait: Jonathan Edwards.
Reproduced by permission of Archive Photos, Inc.

Jonathan Edwards was a Puritan minister and theologian (a specialist in the study of religion) who became one of the principal leaders of the Great Awakening (a series of religious revivals that swept the American colonies near the middle of the eighteenth century). This movement had a profound effect on American politics and society. Protestant preachers from New England to North Carolina, inflamed by the "spirit of God," set out to "wake up" their congregations, whom they accused of sinful behavior. Edwards became famous for the sermon "Sinners in the Hands of an Angry God," in which he terrified his listeners with visions of eternal punishment for unrepentant sinners. Yet Edwards's excessive zeal ultimately led to his undoing. After he imposed harsh rules for admission to his church in Northampton, Massachusetts, he was forced out and sent to a remote Native American mission. During his final years, however, he wrote some of the most important works in American theology.

Shows early intellectual gifts

Jonathan Edwards was born in 1703 in Windsor (now East Windsor), Connecticut. He was the only son of Timothy

Sarah Pierpont Edwards

Sarah Pierpont Edwards was the wife of minister Jonathan Edwards. The daughter of a pastor who founded Yale College, she grew up in a devoutly religious and cultured home. As a teenager she was known for her spirituality and good-natured disposition. In 1727 she married Edwards, and the couple eventually had eleven children (seven daughters and four sons). Throughout her life she kept a diary, which revealed her to be a hardworking, devoted wife. While the Edwardses lived in Northampton, Massachusetts, and Stockbridge, Massachusetts, she was a gracious hostess in her husband's parsonage (a pastor's house), entertaining a steady stream of guests. Once she even prepared eight hundred meals for soldiers stationed at the Indian mission in Stockbridge. Jonathan Edwards was one of the leaders of the Great Awakening, a religious revival that swept New England during the 1730s and 1740s. Like her husband, Sarah Edwards was spiritually transformed by the movement. In her diary she wrote of being "removed from myself," of seeming to "float or swim, in these bright, sweet beams" of "divine love." Sarah died of dysentery six months after Jonathan's death.

Edwards, a clergyman in the Congregational Church, and Ester Stoddard Edwards, daughter of Solomon Stoddard, a famous preacher. At an early age Edwards began to show substantial intellectual gifts. By the time he was twelve years old, for instance, he read the works of English mathematician Isaac Newton and gathered information on rainbows and spiders, which he included in essays he wrote to prove the goodness and wisdom of the Creator (God). Less than a year later he began his studies at Yale College, in New Haven, Connecticut.

A quiet and studious young man, Edwards did not join in the boisterous pranks of his classmates. Instead, he studied the works of English philosopher John Locke and deepened his knowledge of Newton. In 1720 Edwards graduated at the top his class. He remained at Yale for two years of theological study, then preached for a year at a Presbyterian church in New York City. In 1724 he returned to Yale as a tutor. Three years later Edwards joined his grandfather,

Edwards a precocious child

Jonathan Edwards began to show substantial intellectual gifts as a young boy. For instance, he read the works of mathematician Isaac Newton and wrote lengthy essays about rainbows and spiders. Excerpted below is the opening of "The Flying Spider," a description of the web-making genius of spiders, which Edwards composed at age twelve.

> *May it please your Honour [Edwards's teacher],*
>
> *There are some things that I have happily seen of the wondrous way of the working of the spider. Although every thing belonging to this insect is admirable, there are some phenomena relating to them more particularly wonderful. Everybody that is used to the country, knows their marching in the air from one tree to another, sometimes at the distance of five or six rods. Nor can one go out in a dewy morning, at the latter end of August and the beginning of September, but he shall see multitudes of webs, made visible by the dew that hangs on them, reaching from one tree, branch and shrub, to another; which webs are commonly thought to be made in the night, because they appear only in the morning; whereas none of them*

are made in the night, for these spiders never come out in the night when it is dark, as the dew is then falling. But these webs may be seen well enough in the day time by an observing eye, by their reflection in the sunbeams. Especially late in the afternoon, may these webs, that are between the eye and that part of the horizon that is under the sun, be seen very plainly, being advantageously posited [placed] to reflect the rays. And the spiders themselves may very often be seen travelling in the air, from one stage to another amongst the trees, in a very unaccountable manner. But I have often seen that, which is much more astonishing. In very calm and serene days in the fore-mentioned time of year, standing at some distance behind the end of an house or some other opake [opaque] body, so as just to hide the disk of the sun and keep off his dazzling rays, and looking along close by the side of it, I have seen a vast multitude of little shining webs, and glistening strings, brightly reflecting the sunbeams, and some of them of great length, and of such height, that one would think they were tacked to the vault of the heavens. . . .

Reprinted in: Warfel, Harry H., and others, eds. The American Mind: Selections from the Literature of the United States, *Volume I. New York: American Book Co., 1963, p. 82.*

Solomon Stoddard, in the ministry at Northampton, Massachusetts. Around that time he married Sarah Pierpont, daughter of one of the founders of Yale and granddaughter of Thomas Hooker, who established the colony of Connecticut. They were married for over thirty years and had eleven children.

Leads Great Awakening

Upon the death of Stoddard in 1729 Edwards became the leader of the Northampton congregation and soon acquired an enthusiastic following. In 1734 he became involved in the Great Awakening. Edwards described this movement in *A Faithful Narrative of the Surprising Work of God* (1737). One of the other leaders of the Great Awakening was **George Whitefield** (see entry), who was touring the colonies and having considerable success in lifting Christians out of their "lethargy" (lack of religious fervor). Edwards was so impressed with Whitefield that he convinced the reformer to visit Northampton in 1740. Whitefield made a profound impression on Edwards. Although Edwards was not a dramatic actor like Whitefield, he began delivering powerful sermons in which he dwelled more and more on the punishment Christians would suffer if they ignored God's will.

Gives famous sermon

Edwards's "fire and brimstone" approach to salvation reached a peak in 1741, when he delivered his most famous sermon, "Sinners in the Hands of an Angry God." Edwards stunned his listeners with a graphic picture of the uncertain nature of life and the eternal punishment awaiting unrepentant sinners. Now considered a masterpiece of rhetoric (public speaking), "Sinners" bombarded the audience with frightening images of a hell filled with tormented souls who burned eternally like live coals. Edwards compared sinners to a spider dangling from a single silken thread held fast only by God, who would let them drop unless they asked forgiveness. During Whitefield's tour throughout the colonies, Edwards was invited to preach, and each time he presented "Sinners." His audiences were convulsed in "great moaning," crying out, "What shall I do to be saved—oh I am going to Hell!" So intense was their anguish that Edwards had to stop several times whenever he delivered the sermon. He eventually published "Sinners" to great acclaim.

In 1746 Edwards wrote his extensive theological works, *Treatise on Religious Affections,* in which he identified love of God as the fount of all religious feelings. He also wrote a series of pamphlets that defended the intense emotional nature of the Great Awakening. He claimed the movement was

Edwards terrifies "sinners"

Jonathan Edwards's crusade during the Great Awakening reached a peak in 1741, when he delivered his famous sermon, "Sinners in the Hands of an Angry God." He terrified his listeners with a graphic description of the eternal punishment that would await unrepentant sinners. Following is the conclusion of the sermon:

> And let every one that is yet of Christ [Jesus of Nazareth, founder of Christianity], and hanging over the pit of hell, whether they be old men and women, or middle aged, or young people, or little children, now hearken to the loud calls of God's word and providence. This acceptable year of the Lord, a day of such great favors to some, will doubtless be a day of as remarkable vengeance to others. Men's hearts harden, and their guilt increases apace at such a day as this, if they neglect their souls; and never was there so great danger of such persons being given up to hardness of heart and blindness of mind. God seems now to be hastily gathering in his elect [chosen people] in all parts of the land; and probably the greater part of adult persons that ever shall be saved, will be brought in now in a little time, and that it will be as it was on the great out-pouring of the Spirit upon the Jews in the apostles'

> days [the time when followers of Jesus were sent out to teach Christianity to the Jewish people]; the election will obtain [be established], and the rest will be blinded. If this should be the case with you, you will eternally curse this day, and will curse the day that ever you was born, to see such a season of the pouring out of God's Spirit, and will wish that you had died and gone to hell before you had seen it. Now undoubtedly it is, as it was in the days of John the Baptist [a Jewish prophet, considered the forerunner of Christ], the axe is in an extraordinary manner laid at the root of the trees, that every tree which brings not forth good fruit, may be hewn down and cast into the fire.

> Therefore, let every one that is out of Christ, now awake and fly from the wrath to come. The wrath of Almighty God is now undoubtedly hanging over a great part of this congregation: Let every one fly out of Sodom [according to the book of Genesis in the Old Testament, an ancient city destroyed by God because of the wickedness of its inhabitants]: "Haste and escape for your lives, look not behind you, escape to the mountain, lest you be consumed."

Reprinted in: Elliott, Emory, and others, eds. American Literature: A Prentice Hall Anthology. Englewood Cliffs, New Jersey, 1991, p. 311.

a genuine and natural outcome of religious conversion. Critics warned Edwards that he was being irresponsible in judging the spiritual state of others. They condemned his attacks on less fiery clergymen, whom he accused of not being sufficiently inspired by the spirit of God. Yet Edwards shrugged off these charges as insignificant. To him the revivals were the authentic work of God. Energized by the apparent success of the Great

Awakening, Edwards announced that he was reversing his grandfather's policy of admitting any moral person to the church. Under Edwards's new rules, only those who could convince him of their religious conversion would be admitted to his congregation and be allowed to have their children baptized (initiated into the church in a ceremony that involves immersion in water or the sprinkling of water on the head).

Exiled to Stockbridge

Historians have been puzzled about Edwards's reasons for restricting church membership in such a way. The mystery will continue until scholars are able to decipher the handwriting in his notebooks. If he was trying to spark conversions by making parents fear for the souls of their children, the effort backfired. Edwards's congregation rose up against him, appealing to an advisory council of ministers. Nevertheless he refused to recognize the authority of the council. The conflict continued until 1750, when Edwards was finally ousted and sent to Stockbridge, Massachusetts, where he ministered to Native Americans at a remote mission.

Exile in Stockbridge proved to be a blessing. Freed from his pastoral duties, Edwards had the time to think, write, and study. Among the works he published were *A Careful and Strict Enquiry Into . . . Freedom of Will* (1754), *The Great Christian Doctrine of Original Sin Defended* (1758), and *Two Dissertations, I. Concerning the End for which God Created the World. II. The Nature of True Virtue* (published in 1765, after his death). Edwards also wrote treatises in which he argued, among other positions, that humans are not born with knowledge or ideas. Instead, they are granted the faculties to form their own ideas from what their senses tell them about the world, and then have the ability to follow those ideas and do what brings them pleasure. Even today philosophers and theologians are intrigued by the ideas about human nature, God, and religion that Edwards published during this last stage of his life. In 1757 Edwards was offered the position of president of the College of New Jersey (now Princeton University), which was founded by New Side Presbyterians (a branch of Protestantism). He reluctantly accepted the honor, but he died the following year from a smallpox inoculation before he could assume his duties.

For further research

Elliott, Emory, and others, eds. *American Literature: A Prentice Hall Anthology.* Englewood Cliffs, New Jersey, 1991, p. 311.

The Puritans: American Literature Colonial Period (1608-1700). http://falcon.jmu.edu/-ramseyil/amicol.htm Available July 13, 1999.

Tracy, Patricia J. *Jonathan Edwards, Pastor: Religion and Society in Eighteenth-Century Northampton.* New York: Hill & Wang, 1979.

Warfel, Harry H., and others, eds. *The American Mind: Selections from the Literature of the United States,* Volume I. New York: American Book Co., 1963, p. 82.

Winslow, Ola Elizabeth. *Jonathan Edwards: 1703–1758.* New York: Collier Books, 1961.

John Eliot

August 5, 1604
Widford, Hertfordshire, England
May 20, 1690
Roxbury, Massachusetts

Puritan missionary

John Eliot was a Puritan (one who practices strict moral and spiritual codes) missionary known as "the Indian evangelist," or "the Indian Apostle," who devoted his life to converting Native Americans to Christianity. Eliot emigrated from England to the New World (a European term for North America and South America) in 1631. The following year he became a teacher and pastor at the Puritan church in Roxbury, Massachusetts. After learning the Algonquian language, he first preached to Native Americans in 1646. Eliot published many books for his converted or "praying Indians," including a Bible translated into Algonquian in 1663. After Metacom's War (1675–76; also known as King Philip's War), the number of Christian natives dwindled. Eliot's books and achievements still stand, however, as important contributions to colonial American society.

It is "absolutely necessary to carry on civility with religion [for] praying Indians."

John Eliot.

Emigrates to Massachusetts

John Eliot was born in 1604, in Widford, Hertfordshire, England. He was the third of seven children of Bennett and Lettice or Letteye (Aggar) Eliot. His father was a wealthy

Portrait: John Eliot.

101

Native American conversion

During the American colonial period, English settlers made a widespread effort to convert and "civilize" Native Americans in New England and Virginia. Most of the conversions in New England took place in Massachusetts. Missionary John Eliot established fourteen settlements for Christian natives, and published a Bible in the Algonquian language in 1663. One of Eliot's contemporaries, Thomas Mayhew Jr., had converted 283 Native Americans by 1632. Both Eliot and Mayhew were funded by A Corporation for the Promoting and Propagating the Gospel among the Indians of New England, a religious missionary organization established in London, England, in 1649. Native American conversion thrived in Massachusetts until it was stifled by King Philip's War (1675–76). There were almost no missions in Connecticut until 1726, when **Cotton Mather** (see entry) founded a school on the Mohegan reserve.

In Virginia, the English mission to convert Native Americans began promisingly enough when Reverend Alexander Whitaker converted the Powhatan "princess" **Pocahontas** (see entry) to Christianity. Her subsequent visit to England led to the establishment of an Indian college at Henrico, a project that collapsed after the massacre of settlers around Jamestown in 1622. The College of William and Mary was established in 1693, with one instructor to teach Native Americans. Although few Native Americans attended the college, it remained open with money from a fund established by scientist Robert Boyle. A statement by Massachusetts governor Robert Dinwiddie reflects the attitude of the settlers toward the education of Native Americans. In 1756 Dinwiddie wrote that they had "no inclination to learning" and "could not be reconciled to their books."

landowner with property in Eastwick, Hundson, Ware, and Widford. Eliot began attending Jesus College at Cambridge University in 1619. An excellent scholar of the classics (Greek and Roman literature), he received a bachelor's degree in 1622. Eliot then began teaching at a grammar school in Little Baddam, Essex. The school was run by Thomas Hooker, a Puritan minister who eventually became pastor of First Church at Cambridge, Massachusetts. Hooker's Puritanism was a major influence on Eliot, who decided to become a preacher.

Although Eliot dutifully abided by the laws of the Church of England (or Anglican Church; the official religion in England), his newfound Puritanism came into conflict with the religious beliefs he had been taught as a child. Consequently he decided to leave for the New World, where he was free to become a Puritan. Eliot sailed on board the *Lyon*, arriving at Boston, Massachusetts, on November 4, 1631. He was accompanied by members of the family of colonist **John Winthrop** (see entry). Three of Eliot's brothers and three of his sisters came along as well. Before leaving England, Eliot had become engaged to Ann (or Hannah) Mumford, who joined him in Massachusetts a year later. They were married on September 4, 1632, and later had six children.

In Boston, Eliot worked as a substitute teacher for John Wilson, who was visiting England. Eliot was asked to continue teaching after Wilson's return. However, when more of Eliot's former countrymen emigrated to Roxbury, Massachusetts, they invited him to come and join them there. According to Winthrop's *History* (a history of the Massachusetts Bay Colony), Eliot was popular in Boston: "though Boston laboured all they could, both with the congregation of Roxbury and with Mr. Eliot himself . . . he could not be diverted from accepting the call of Roxbury." After declining the offer to teach in Boston, Eliot joined the new English emigrants in Roxbury. They made him a teacher and pastor of their church in 1632, and he remained there until the end of his life.

Converts Native Americans

At Roxbury, Eliot began his campaign to convert local Native Americans to Christianity. Adept at learning languages, he spent two years studying Native American dialects with an interpreter. Eliot first preached to Native Americans on October 28, 1646, at a settlement called Nonantum. He delivered the sermon in the local dialect, but prayed in English. Eliot had such success in converting Native Americans that in 1649 A Corporation for the Promoting and Propagating the Gospel among the Indians of New England was established in England to fund his endeavors. The first order for the advancement of Native American learning was passed on March 17,1647.

As part of the education process, Eliot believed that the converted Native Americans should be independent from the

John Eliot preaching to the Native Americans.
Reproduced by permission of The Granger Collection Ltd.

American settlers. With money from London, he built settlements where Christianized Native Americans lived in houses, wore European-style clothes, and owned land. Most important, Eliot envisioned that the settlements would be self-governing. Native Americans would be free to manage their own affairs under the jurisdiction of the general laws of Massachusetts. In 1651 the first town of "praying Indians" was established at Natick. The first Native American church was also founded at Natick in 1660 and was active until 1716.

Publishes Bible

After founding Natick, Eliot frequently traveled back and forth between the new settlement and Roxbury. In addition to fulfilling his responsibilities as pastor of the Roxbury church, Eliot prepared religious materials for the converted Native Americans. He translated works from English into the local dialect so they could be easily read by the converts. His earliest translation was a catechism (a summary or religious doctrine often in the form of questions and answers) published in Native American dialect in 1653. He also provided a book of psalms (sacred songs or poems used in worship) in translation five years later. Eliot's largest project was a translation of the Bible into Algonquian. Funded by the London organization, printing began in 1658. A translation of the New Testament was published in 1661. When a translation of the Old Testament arrived in 1663, Eliot's Algonquian Bible was complete. This was the first Bible to be printed in North America.

Efforts hindered by war

Eliot continued to believe that the Christian natives should lead separate and independent lives. He even trained several Native Americans as preachers, thinking they would be better missionaries for their people. Eliot made progress with this endeavor, and there were twenty-four Native American preachers by the time he died. However, not everyone agreed with Eliot's efforts. For instance, during his travels throughout New England he encountered opposition from Native Americans. Metacom's War further stifled Eliot's progress. This devastating conflict between the colonists and the Wampanoags broke out when a Christian Native American was murdered, possibly on orders from the Wampanoag chief **Metacom** (see entry). Although many Christian Native Americans fought for the English, they found themselves in a difficult position. Mistrusted by the Puritans, they were also under suspicion from other Native Americans. Eliot himself was held under suspicion for his efforts at segregation (separation of Native Americans from colonists). As a result, the number of Christian natives began to decline. In 1674, before the war, there had been about thiry-six hundred converts, and fourteen settlements. Following the war, the number of settlements dropped to four and the number of Christianized Native Americans significantly decreased.

Gives land for natives and slaves

Although Eliot's conversion work came to a virtual halt, his books seem to have had a lasting impact. In 1659 he published *The Christian Commonwealth*, which was condemned by the English government because it promoted republicanism (self-government). Ten years later Eliot released *The Indian Primer,* a grammar book for the Native American dialect. In addition to his effort to create a society of Christian natives, Eliot served as a witness during the trial of religious enthusiast **Anne Hutchinson** (see entry) in 1637. Eliot is remembered for one of his last deeds, which was to provide land for Native Americans and African Americans in Roxbury. Eliot died in Roxbury on May 20, 1690.

For further research

Johnson, Allen, and others, eds. *Dictionary of American Biography.* New York: Scribner, 1946–1958, pp. 79–80.

Stephen, Leslie, and Sidney Lee, eds. *The Dictionary of National Biography.* London, England: Oxford University Press, 1917, pp. 607–12.

Winslow, Ola Elizabeth. *John Eliot: Apostle to the Indians.* Boston: Houghton Mifflin, 1968.

John Endecott

1588 (or 1589)
Dorchester, England
March 15, 1665
Boston, Massachusetts

Governor and military leader

John Endecott was one of the early leaders of the Massachusetts Bay Colony, which consisted of several settlements and towns. He came to the New World (the European term for North and South America) in 1628 as a member of a small group that paved the way for the "Great Migration" of Puritans (a religious group who preached strict moral and spiritual codes) two years later. Endecott was a strict Puritan whose actions generally benefitted the colony. Nevertheless, he could also be extremely cruel, and he dealt very harshly with dissenters (those who question authority) and other rebels. He is infamous for cutting down the maypole at Merry Mount (now Quincy) to punish unruly settlers. (A maypole is a tall flower-wreathed pole that is the center for May Day sports and dances, which were not condoned by Puritans.) Endecott is best known, however, for the expedition that led to the Pequot War of 1636 and for his harsh treatment of Quakers (members of the Religious Society of Friends who believe that the individual can receive divine truth from the Holy Spirit through his or her own "inner light" without the guidance of a minister or priest) toward the end of 1660. The strong-willed Endecott served as governor until his death in 1665.

John Endecott "rebuked the inhabitants [of the Massachusetts Bay Colony] for their profaneness, and admonished them to look to it that they walked better."

Puritan leader John Winthrop.

Portrait: John Endecott.
Reproduced by permission of Archive Photos, Inc.

Helps form Puritan colony

John Endecott was born in 1588 (or 1589) in Dorchester, England. His parents were Thomas and Alice (Westlake) Endecott. His grandfather was a wealthy man who held mining interests in England. As a young man, Endecott became a Puritan after being influenced by the Reverend John White of Dorchester and the Reverend Samuel Shelton, who became the pastor of the First Church in Salem, Massachusetts. Because of his conversion, Endecott was practically disowned by his grandfather, who disagreed with his religious views. Before emigrating (moving from one country to another) to the New World, Endecott married Ann Gower, who was related to Matthew Craddock, the governor of the Massachusetts Bay Colony in England (at that time the colonies did not have self-rule).

Endecott had no trouble finding other Puritans who were interested in emigrating to New England. By 1628 the Plymouth Colony had already been well established, and there were some settlers in the Massachusetts Bay Colony. On March 19, 1628, Endecott joined six other "religious persons" in purchasing a patent (an official document giving a right or privilege) from the Plymouth Council (the British government agency that issued colonizing rights) for land in the Massachusetts Bay Colony. With permission to colonize, the group proceeded immediately to the New World. On June 20, 1628, Endecott and his wife joined about thirty other emigrants and sailed out of Weymouth, England on board the ship *Abigail*. After reaching Naumkeag (now Salem), Massachusetts, on September 6, 1628, the small group prepared for other settlers who were to come later. Ann Endecott died soon after they arrived in Massachusetts, and John Endecott was remarried in 1630 to Elizabeth Gibson. They had two sons.

Punishes rebels and dissenters

Historians have difficulty in determining Endecott's title after he landed at Massachusetts. On April 30, 1629, he was appointed temporary governor by the Plymouth Company in England. His election, some sources say, was probably influenced by his relation to Craddock. On October 20, 1629, **John Winthrop** (see entry) was elected the official governor of Massachusetts, but he did not arrive in the colony until 1630. As a result, Endecott headed Plymouth for an entire year. Even though Endecott initially held the position, historians consider Winthrop the first official governor of the Massachusetts Bay Colony.

While Endecott was in office he made considerable progress in clearing the way for more settlers. For instance, he commanded a military company that protected settlers against Native Americans. But Native Americans were not the only problem. The colonists also had to confront merchants and planters who had already settled the area. Endecott had the most problems with the traders in Mount Wollaston, or Merry Mount. He disapproved of the conduct of **Thomas Morton** (see entry), who headed a gang of traders. Leading an expedition to Merry Mount, Endecott "rebuked the inhabitants for their profaneness," and admonished them to "look to it that they walked better." In an event now famous in American history, Endecott cut down the maypole at Merry Mount to discourage such public celebrations as dancing and sporting events.

As temporary governor, Endecott also had to deal with religious problems in Massachusetts. After Puritan preachers Samuel Skelton and Francis Higginson arrived in 1629, a new church was built for the colony. Calling themselves Separatists (those that separated from the Church of England), Endecott and the two clergymen organized a church that was based on the one in Plymouth and separate from the Puritan church in England. When two colonists, John and Samuel Browne, refused to become Separatists, Endecott deported them to England. Although British authorities were generally satisfied with Endecott's job as governor, they were critical of his treatment of the Brownes. His abrupt actions revealed an intolerance toward dissenters and foreshadowed his eventual harsh treatment of the Quakers.

Reveals extreme Puritanism

The summer of 1630 marked the high point of the "Great Migration" of Puritans to New England. Nearly one thousand new settlers arrived from England. Among them was Winthrop, who brought a charter (a grant or guarantee from the sovereign power of a state or country) that allowed the New England settlers to govern themselves. Winthrop immediately took over as governor and Endecott willingly gave up his position to become Winthrop's assistant. In return for his

The "Great Migration" and the Pequot War

As a result of the "Great Migration" of Puritans to New England, the population of the Massachusetts Bay Colony rose from about 4,000 to 11,000 between 1634 and 1638. In 1635 Puritans moved west onto land that was controlled by the Pequots, a Native American tribe. For instance, the Hartford settlement was established by Baptist minister Thomas Hooker, and Fort Saybrook was built by the English Saybrook Company near the Pequot village of Mystic. Because the English were allied with their enemies, the Naragansetts, the Pequots were not friendly with the English. As the Puritans began their westward expansion, tensions increased between the colonists and the Pequots.

The Puritans' main goal was to rid the area of all Native Americans. Even though the colonists had a treaty with the Pequots, they hoped to provoke the Native Americans into breaking the agreement. When Native Americans from an unknown tribe killed two English colonists, John Stone and John Oldham, colonists had the provocation they wanted. In September 1636, Endecott led an attack on the Pequots and their allies on Block Island, thus beginning the Pequot War. After the Pequots retaliated by laying siege to Fort Saybrook, the conflict quieted for some time. Western settlers worried that the Pequots would be victorious, however, and fighting soon escalated. The war finally ended at Mystic after the settlers burned the village and exterminated nearly all the Pequots. The few survivors were either killed later by the Puritans or they fled to other parts of the country. In 1638 the Treaty of Hartford declared the Pequot nation to be dissolved.

services, Endecott was granted land in 1632, and two years later he was appointed military commissioner of the colony.

Endecott continued making history, even as an assistant to the governor. In September 1634 he cut the cross of St. George from a banner used by the colonists in Salem. Being a strict Puritan, Endecott believed that the cross represented popery. ("Popery" refers to the pope, the head of the Roman Catholic Church. Puritans opposed any symbol of the Catholic Church.) Although the Puritan community, including Winthrop, secretly sympathized with his actions, the matter was brought before the general court in 1635. Endecott was suspended from office for one year. He was reappointed assistant governor in 1636. During the same year two colonists, John Stone and John Oldham, were killed by Native Americans from an unknown tribe. In retaliation, Endecott led an expedition against the Pequot Indians that resulted in the Pequot War. Also in 1636, the military finally agreed that the cross of St. George was idolatrous (the worship of a physical object as a god) and should be left off the colony's banners.

Becomes official governor

After 1636 Endecott held various positions in the government of the Massachusetts Bay Colony. When Winthrop died on March 29, 1649, Endecott took his place as governor. He was reelected governor every year until his death, except for 1650 and 1654, when he served as deputy governor.

As governor Endecott enforced strict Puritan principles, and he felt that it was his duty to punish dissenters. He had problems particularly with the Quakers, who believed that church leaders should have no role in determining whether individual Christians had gained salvation (forgiveness of sins against God). In 1659 Endecott executed Quaker dissenters William Robinson and Marmaduke Stephenson. Then in 1660 he executed Quaker rebel **Mary Dyer** (see entry), who had repeatedly defied the community's laws against Quaker activities. Some historians believe that Endecott was too brutal in his handling of rebels such as Robinson, Stephenson, and Dyer. However, other scholars point to the prevailing opinion among colonists that dissenters should be executed.

After 1660 the Massachusetts Bay Colony struggled to preserve its freedom. As governor, Endecott petitioned King Charles II in England, begging for protection and continued liberty for colonists. Charles II decided to send four commissioners to investigate the Massachusetts government and court. When the commissioners returned to England they issued a highly negative report to the king. On October 19, 1664, Endecott wrote to Secretary William Morrice protesting the power of the commissioners. Morrice, in turn, complained to the king about Endecott's conduct and recommended that he be replaced. Before a new governor was appointed, however, Endecott died in Boston on March 15, 1665.

Shows humanity with interest in education

Despite his flaws, Endecott managed to be a successful governor until his death because he was strong-willed. Most historians agree that Endecott was self-absorbed and cruel to dissenters. Yet others point out that circumstances at the time demanded such a man. To say that Endecott was completely inhumane would be to ignore the fact that he supported education for the colonists. In 1641 he suggested establishing a free school in Salem. In 1642 he became a member of the staff at Harvard College in Cambridge, Massachusetts. Endecott was survived by his son John and his other son Zerubbabel, who was a physician in Salem.

For further research

Johnson, Allen, and others, eds. *Dictionary of American Biography.* New York: Scribner, pp. 155–57.

Stephen, Leslie, and Sidney Lee, eds. *The Dictionary of National Biography.* London, England: Oxford University Press, 1917, pp. 784–87.

Olaudah Equiano

c. 1745
Nigeria, Africa
1797
England

Freedman, sailor, author, and abolitionist

Olaudah Equiano (pronounced ek-wee-ANH-o; also known as Gustavus Vassa) led a remarkable life as a slave and freedman. The son of an African chief, he was captured at age eleven by African slave traders. After being sold to European traders, Equiano was sent first to the Caribbean. He was then transported to a plantation in Virginia, where he was bought by British naval officer Michael Henry Pascal. While serving Pascal, he received many advantages such as being taught how to read and write English. He also became a skillful sailor during the Seven Years War (1756–63; a worldwide conflict between major European powers). After the war, Equiano was traded to Robert King. King provided Equiano with the experience to begin his own trading business, which enabled him to save enough money to buy his freedom in 1766. After writing *The Interesting Narrative of the Life of Olaudah Equiano* (1789), Equiano became an influential abolitionist (a person who takes measures to end slavery).

Becomes Virginia plantation slave

It is believed that Olaudah Equiano was born in Nigeria, Africa, in 1745. He was the son of the chief of the East-

"The next day proved a day of greater sorrow than I had yet experienced; for my sister and I were then separated, while we lay clasped in each other's arms."

From The Interesting Narrative of the Life of Olaudah Equiano.

Portrait: Olaudah Equiano.
Reproduced by permission of the New York Historical Society.

113

Equiano and sister kidnapped

In *The Interesting Narrative of the Life of Olaudah Equiano* (1789), Olaudah Equiano described how he and his sister were kidnapped by African slave traders.

One day, when all our people were gone out to their works as usual, and only I and my dear sister were left to mind the house, two men and woman got over our walls, and in a moment seized us both; and, without giving us time to cry out, or to make resistance, they stopped our mouths, tied our hands, and ran off with us into the nearest wood, and continued to carry us as far as they could, till night came on, when we reached a small house, where the robbers halted for refreshment, and spent the night.

We were then unbound, but were unable to take any food; and, being quite overpowered by fatigue and grief, our only relief was some sleep, which allayed [reduced] our misfortune for a short time. The next morning we left the house, and continued travelling all the day. For a long time we had kept to the woods, but at last we came into a road which I believed I knew. I now had some hopes of being delivered, for we had advanced but a little way before I discovered some people at a distance, on which I began to cry out for their assistance; but my cries had no other effect than to make them tie me faster, and stop my mouth, and then they put me into a large sack. They also stopped my sister's mouth, and tied her hands. And in this manner we proceeded till we were out of the sight of these people.

When we went to rest the following night they offered us some victuals [food], but we refused them; and the only comfort we had was in being in one another's arms all that night, and bathing each other in our tears. But, alas! we were soon deprived of even the smallest comfort of weeping together. The next day proved a day of greater sorrow than I had yet experienced; for my sister and I were then separated, while we lay clasped in each other's arms. It was in vain that we besought them not to part us: she was torn from me, and immediately carried away, while I was left in a state of distraction not to be described. I cried and grieved continually; and for several days I did not eat anything but what they forced into my mouth.

Later Equiano's sister was brought to a house where he was working as a slave, and he was overjoyed to see her. But, he said, " . . . she was again torn from me forever! I was now more miserable, if possible, than before. . . . "

Reprinted in: Stiles, T. J., ed. In Their Own Words: The Colonizers. *New York: Berkeley Publishing Group, 1998, pp. 352–53, 354.*

Nigerian Ibo tribe who probably lived near present-day Onitsha. As a child, Equiano experienced the security of tribal unity. This world was shattered, however, when he and his sister were captured by African tribesmen who participated in the slave trade. After being separated from his sister, Equiano was

traded from village to village in Africa, where he worked for a variety of masters. Eventually taken to the coast of West Africa, Equiano was purchased by a European slave master. He was transported thousands of miles to the Caribbean island of Barbados, whose sugar plantations made it the richest British colony during the eighteenth century. Chained to many other captives in the hot, stinking hold of a slave ship, Equiano witnessed firsthand the brutal treatment of slaves by European traders. When none of the planters in Barbados purchased Equiano, he was taken to Virginia and put to work on a tobacco plantation.

Starts business, buys freedom

Only a few weeks after being purchased in Virginia, Equiano was sold again to a lieutenant in the Royal Navy, Michael Henry Pascal. While serving Pascal, Equiano received many advantages that improved his life in the New World

Before buying his freedom, Equiano worked as a plantation slave like the slaves on this Virginia plantation. *Reproduced by permission of the Granger Collection Ltd.*

(European term for North and South America). It was Pascal who named Equiano after the sixteenth-century Swedish king Gustavus I. While sailing with Pascal to England in 1757, Equiano met a Virginian named Richard Baker, who taught him to read and write. Equiano subsequently took every opportunity to improve his reading and writing skills and to add to his knowledge. In 1759, while visiting London, England, one of Pascal's friends had Equiano baptized (initiated into Christianity) at St. Margaret's Church, in Westminster.

During the Seven Years War, Pascal permitted Equiano to become a skillful sailor. He served on many naval vessels in the Atlantic Ocean and the Mediterranean Sea and even held an important position during his service. For instance, he was a steward (an employee on a ship who manages the provisioning of food and attends passengers) on board the *Aetna* in 1761. After the war Equiano was promised his freedom. When he asked to be set free, however, Pascal was so angered by the request that he sent Equiano back to the West Indies to be sold as a slave. Fortunately, this time he was sold to a merchant named Robert King, who was a Quaker (member of a religious group that believed in personal communication with the Holy Spirit; Quakers also opposed slavery).

Equiano proved quite valuable to King because of his skills as a sailor as well as his ability to read, write, and calculate. Equiano assisted King in shipping sugar and other agricultural goods between the Caribbean, Georgia, and South Carolina. Once, Equiano was even forced to transport slaves. Despite the fact that the Quakers had renounced (rejected) slavery as part of their religion in 1761, King still required Equiano to buy his freedom. While sailing from port to port for King, Equiano began a small trading business of his own. He saved his money, and by 1766 he had accumulated enough to purchase his freedom.

Becomes prominent abolitionist

In the decade after his emancipation (freedom), Equiano continued to work as a sailor on merchant ships and visited various American ports. While in Savannah, Georgia, he attended a service led by English evangelist **George Whitefield** (see entry). The clergyman's powerful sermon inspired Equiano to thinking about heaven, hell, and salvation, thoughts that troubled him for several years. Finally, in 1774, he experienced a religious conversion while visiting Cadiz, Spain. This experience resulted in a less anxious nature and instilled in him a desire for worship and Bible reading that brought him into contact with other Christians. He also decided that the slave trade was immoral and should be abolished. In England and in the colonies, he met Quakers, Anglicans, and Methodists who shared his determination to end slavery.

Equiano became an important contact person for the early abolitionists. Traveling between England and America, he carried news of the horrors of slavery and informed sympathetic listeners about the courage of antislavery activists. With the publication of his autobiography, *The Interesting Narrative of the Life of Olaudah Equiano,* Equiano became an influential spokesman for the abolition of slavery. Nine editions of his book were printed during his lifetime, and it brought him international fame. In this narrative, Equiano compares the slaves with the Hebrews in the Bible, and presents many antislavery views. As a result, the book is considered one of the best precursors to slave narratives such as the *Narrative of the Life of Frederick Douglass* (1845) and others that were written around the time of the American Civil War (1861–65; the Civil War was a conflict between Northern states and Southern states, which formed an independent Confederacy, over complex economic and social issues, including slavery).

Marries an Englishwoman

In addition to his trading missions, Equiano took on other adventures during his lifetime. In 1772–73, he joined an expedition to the Arctic and later toured the Mediterranean as a servant. He was also an assistant to a doctor with the Miskito Indians in Nicaragua. In 1777, Equiano settled in the British Isles, where he became an active abolitionist. During a journey to Philadelphia, Pennsylvania, in 1785, he was pleased to observe that the Quakers had emancipated slaves and founded a free school in the city. In 1792, he married an Englishwoman, Susan Cullen, with whom he had two daughters, Anna Maria and Johanna. Susan Cullen Vassa died only months after Johanna's birth, and Equiano died in 1797. Johanna died two months after her father, but Anna Maria survived into adulthood.

For further research

Cameron, Ann. *The Kidnaped Prince: The Life of Olaudah Equiano.* New York: Knopf, 1995.

Gates, Henry Louis Jr., ed. *The Classic Slave Narratives.* New York: New American Library, 1987.

Johnson, Charles, Patricia Smith, and WGBH Research Team, eds. *Africans in America: America's Journey through Slavery.* New York: Harcourt, Brace & Company, 1998.

"Olaudah Equiano." http://www.atomicage.com/equiano/life.html Available July 13, 1999.

Stiles, T. J., ed. *In Their Own Words: The Colonizers.* New York: Berkeley Publishing Group, 1998, pp. 352–53, 354.

Estevanico

c. 1500
Azemmour, Morocco
1539
Hawikuh (a Zuni pueblo in New Mexico)

Explorer and "medicine man"

Estevanico (also known as Estevan, Estebanico, or Esteban) was a Moroccan slave who, along with an expedition of Spanish explorers, traveled from Florida along the Gulf of Mexico into the southwestern United States. He was captured by Native Americans and escaped to become a successful "medicine man" (a priestly healer). After an epic journey he finally reached the Spanish outpost of Mexico City. Estevanico was the first Westerner to reach some areas of the southwestern United States. He preceded Spanish conquistador **Francisco Vásquez de Coronado** (see entry) in visiting the "Seven Cities of Cíbola," seven pueblos (Native American villages) in northern Mexico legendary for their mythical riches. Estevanico was killed there by Zuni warriors.

Taken to Spain as slave

At the beginning of the sixteenth century, when Estevanico was born, the Arabs of Morocco were in constant warfare with their Spanish and Portuguese neighbors to the north. During one of these conflicts, Estevanico was captured and sold as a slave in Spain. The Spanish often referred to him as

"After [Estevanico] had left the friars, he thought he could get all the reputation and honor himself, and that if he should discover those settlements with such famous high houses, alone, he would be considered bold and courageous."

Pedro de Casteñeda Estevanico.

Portrait: Estevanico.
Reproduced by permission of The Granger Collection, New York.

Was Estevanico a black African?

Estevanico is a fascinating figure for historians who have attempted to unravel the mysteries of his life. One of the most important controversies concerns Estevanico's "race." Chroniclers from the sixteenth century, who were contemporaries of Estevanico, considered him a Negro (a term used in the past for a black person). However, modern historians claim he was descended from the Hamites, who were Caucasians (a term for white people) living in Africa. Consequently, he could not be a black African. Historian Carroll L. Riley asserts that Estevanico was "Black in the sense that we would use the word in modern America . . . . Actually, in modern generic terms I suspect that Esteban was very mixed." She also explains that if he was considered a Negro, his mixture must have been mainly black. In addition, historians point to other evidence, including his personality and colorful dress, as well as the fact that, like most black Africans, he is often overlooked in historical accounts.

"Estevanico the Black." Estevanico may well have been descended in part from black Africans, since for many years the Arabs and Berbers (native Caucasian people of North Africa) had contact with blacks who lived south of the Sahara Desert. Estevanico came into the possession of Andrés Dorantes de Carranca, a Spanish nobleman. Taking Estevanico as his servant, Carranca joined the expedition to North America led by Spanish explorer Pánfilo de Narváez. Another Spaniard, Álvar Núñez Cabeza de Vaca, who would later become one of the most famous explorers of North America, also took part in this voyage.

Goes to North America

In April 1528, the Spanish ships landed on the Florida coast. Disregarding the advice of his captains, Narváez abandoned the ships and marched into Florida on May 1 in search of gold. According to the report that Cabeza de Vaca made after his return to Spain, Narváez's expedition was attacked by Native Americans near the site of present-day Tallahassee, Florida. The Spaniards went to a bay on the Gulf of Mexico and constructed five boats, with which they hoped to travel along the coastline to a Spanish outpost in Mexico. Setting sail on September 22, 1528, Estevanico was in the boat commanded by Dorantes de Carranca.

In November the small fleet was hit by violent storms. Dorantes de Carranca's boat and the one captained by Cabeza de Vaca were wrecked, possibly on Galveston Island or Mustang Island, off the coast of Texas. The survivors spent the winter on the island, and by spring 1529 only fifteen men were still alive.

Thirteen of them, including Estevanico, left Galveston to try to reach Mexico by walking overland. Cabeza de Vaca was too sick to travel and was left behind, presumably to die.

Captured in Texas

The party led by Dorantes de Carranca headed west and south. Several men died along the way. The rest, including Dorantes de Carranca and Estevanico, were captured by Native Americans at San Antonio Bay on the Texas coast. They were harshly treated by their captors, and by the autumn of 1530 only Dorantes de Carranca, Estevanico, and Alonzo de Castillo were still alive. Dorantes de Carranca managed to escape, traveling inland to a village of the Mariame tribe, where he was held in captivity. In spring 1532, Estevanico and Castillo also escaped and joined Dorantes de Carranca at the Mariame village.

Meets Cabeza de Vaca

During the winter of the following year, Estevanico and the others were surprised to encounter Cabeza de Vaca. He had not only survived but had been working as a trader among the various Native American tribes. The four Europeans were not allowed to stay together, but they planned to meet and then make their escape in the autumn at the annual Native American festival to celebrate the harvest of prickly pears. In September 1534, the four men managed to flee from a site near the present-day city of San Antonio, Texas. They encountered a camp of the Avavares tribe, where they were warmly welcomed as medicine men with special powers, probably because of their foreign appearance.

Becomes known as a medicine man

Estevanico, Cabeza de Vaca, Dorantes de Carranca, and Castillo performed healing rituals for the Native Americans. Estevanico was especially noted for his ability to learn other languages and to use sign language. When the four men left the Avavares in spring 1535, they found that their reputation as healers had preceded them, and they were welcomed wherever they went. As they traveled west, they saw evidence of many different cultures. Visiting the Pueblo tribes of the area

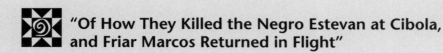

"Of How They Killed the Negro Estevan at Cibola, and Friar Marcos Returned in Flight"

Pedro de Casteñeda, a member of the Coronado expedition, recorded a Zuni eyewitness account of the killing of Estevanico in *The Narrative of the Expedition of Coronado* (published 1896).

After Estevan had left the friars, he thought he could get all the reputation and honor himself, and that if he should discover those settlements with such famous high houses, alone, he would be considered bold and courageous. So he proceeded with the people who had followed him, and attempted to cross the wilderness which lies between the country he had passed through and Cibola. He was so far ahead of the friars that, when these reached Chichilticalli [a city near the Gila River in present-day Arizona], which is on the edge of the wilderness, he was already at Cibola, which is eighty leagues beyond. [One league equals 2.4 to 4.6 miles.] It is 220 leagues from Culican [a city in northwestern Mexico] to the edge of the wilderness, and eighty across the desert, which makes 300, or perhaps ten more or less. As I said, Estevan reached Cibola loaded with the large quantity of turquoises they had given him and some beautiful women whom the Indians who followed him and carried his things were taking with them and had given him. These had followed him from all the settlements he had passed, believing that under his protection they could traverse the whole world without any danger. But as the people in this country were more intelligent than those who followed Estevan, they lodged him in a little hut they had outside

that is now New Mexico, they saw metal bells and medicine gourds the Pueblos had made. Estevanico kept one of the gourds to use in his healing rituals. When they reached the Rio Grande (a river that runs between Texas and Mexico) at the end of 1535, Castillo and Estevanico headed upstream. They came upon the permanent towns (pueblos) of the Jumano tribe. When Cabeza de Vaca and Dorantes de Carranca joined Castillo and Estevanico, they found Estevanico surrounded by Native Americans, who treated him like a god.

Scouts trail to Cíbola

As they traveled toward Mexico, the men heard tales of a group of fabulously rich cities located there, called the Seven Cities of Cíbola. From the Rio Grande, Estevanico and the three Spaniards trekked into what is now the Mexican state of Chihuahua. As they moved south, they began to see more and more evidence that other Europeans were exploring the area.

their village, and the older men and the governors heard his story and took steps to find out the reason he had come to that country. For three days they made inquiries about him and held a council. The account which the negro gave them of two white men who were following him, sent by a great lord, who knew about the things in the sky, and how these were coming to instruct them in divine matters, made them think that he must be a spy or a guide from some nations who wished to come and conquer them, because it seemed to them unreasonable to say that the people were white in the country from which he came and that he was sent by them, he being black. Besides these other reasons, they thought it was hard of him to ask them for turquoises and women, and so they decided to kill him. They did this, but they did not kill any of those who went with him, although they kept some young fellows and let the others, about sixty persons, return freely to their own country. As these, who were badly scared, were returning in flight, they happened to come upon the friars in the desert sixty leagues from Cibola, and told them the sad news, which frightened them so much that they would not even trust these folks who had been with the negro, but opened the packs they were carrying and gave away everything they had except the holy vestments for saying mass. They returned from here by double marches, prepared for anything, without seeing any more of the country except what the Indians told them.

Reprinted in: Gunn, Giles, ed. Early American Writing. New York: Penguin, 1994, pp. 48–49.

For instance, they met a party of Spaniards in March 1536. Finally, they reached Tenochtitlán (present-day Mexico City) the following July, more than eight years after they had landed on the Florida coast. Viceroy (governor) Antonio de Mendoza welcomed the three Spaniards and Estevanico in Mexico, treating them to generous hospitality. Eventually Dorantes de Carranca sold or gave Estevanico to Mendoza. Intrigued by the tales Cabeza de Vaca told of wealthy cities to the north, the viceroy commissioned an expedition to find the Seven Cities of Cíbola. He accepted the offer of a Spanish friar (a member of a religious order) Fray Marcos de Niza to lead the exploring party, and he appointed Estevanico to be a guide.

Estevanico and Fray Marcos began their journey on March 7, 1539. Two weeks later Fray Marcos decided to camp while Estevanico went ahead to scout the trail. After four days Native American messengers informed Fray Marcos that Estevanico had heard news that he was within a thirty days' march from Cíbola and he wanted Fray Marcos to join him. Fray Marcos immediately started northward, but Estevanico did not wait for him. As the friar entered each new village, he found a message from Estevanico saying that he had continued onward. Fray Marcos chased after him for weeks but was unable to catch up.

Estevanico went through the vast desert region of the Mexican state of Sonora and the area that is now southern Arizona. He was the first Westerner to enter the area of Arizona and New Mexico. In May, he reached the Zuni pueblo of Hawikuh, which was supposedly the first of the Seven Cities of Cíbola.

Killed by Zunis

Wherever he traveled, Estevanico sent his medicine gourd ahead of him with Native American messengers to announce his arrival. Usually this token assured him a friendly welcome. At Hawikuh, however, the reception was not as warm as he had expected. When he displayed his "magic" gourd, the Zuni chief threw it down in anger. Then the chief took all of Estevanico's possessions and put him in a house on the edge of the town without food or water. The next morning Estevanico was attacked by warriors and killed.

When the Zuni were later asked why they had killed Estevanico, they said he had claimed there was a huge army coming behind him with many weapons. Meeting in council, the chiefs decided he was a spy and that the safest course of action was to kill him. After Estevanico was dead, his body was cut into pieces and distributed among the chiefs. Several of Estevanico's Native American escorts escaped the Zuni village. When they found Fray Marcos they gave him the news of Estevanico's death.

Marcos finds Estevanico's belongings

Later, in a report to Mendoza, Fray Marcos said he traveled north until he could see Hawikuh, or Cíbola, but that he did not enter the pueblo. He described it as a rich place, even grander than Mexico City. Since Hawikuh was in fact only a small pueblo, Fray Marcos most likely lied about seeing the town. His report inspired Mendoza to send out another expedition led by Coronado. When Coronado's party reached the small village of Hawikuh, the only traces of Estevanico they found were his green dinner plates, his greyhound dogs, and his metal bells. All of these items were now in the possession of the Zuni chief.

For further research

"Estevanico the Moor." http://www.thehistorynet.com/AmericanHistory/articles/1997/0897_text.html Available July 13, 1999.

The Estevanico Society. http://www.estevanico.org/ Available July 13, 1999.

Gunn, Giles, ed. *Early American Writing.* New York: Penguin, 1994, pp. 48–49.

Parish, Helen Rand. *Estebanico.* New York: Viking Press, 1974. (Fiction)

Terrell, John Upton. *Estevanico the Black.* Los Angeles: Westernlore Press, 1968.

Benjamin Franklin

January 17, 1706
Boston, Massachusetts
April 17, 1790
Philadelphia, Pennsylvania

Scientist, inventor, author, philosopher, and one of the founding fathers of the United States

"God helps them that help themselves."

From Benjamin Franklin's Poor Richard's Almanack.

Portrait: Benjamin Franklin.
Reproduced by permission of the Library of Congress.

Throughout his lifetime Benjamin Franklin held many positions, including printer, writer, civic leader, inventor, politician, and ambassador. During the colonial period, he gained international recognition for his experiments and writings on electricity. In fact, he was the most famous scientist of his time. Before Franklin, electricity was considered a bizarre and misunderstood force. His numerous investigations established the study of electricity as a valid scientific pursuit. A native Bostonian, Franklin moved to Philadelphia, Pennsylvania, at the age of seventeen. He started his own printing business and retired a rich man in 1748. Pursuing a wide range of scientific interests, his annual *Poor Richard's Almanack* provided a wealth of information about stars and planets, advice about medicine, weather predictions, and rhymes and witty sayings. In 1744 Franklin founded the American Philosophical Society, the first scientific organization in America. Later in life, his diplomatic work helped the United States develop relationships with European countries, especially France.

Becomes an apprentice

Benjamin Franklin was born on January 17, 1706, in Boston, Massachusetts. His father was Josiah Franklin and his mother was Abiah Folger. Because his family was poor, the young Franklin did not receive a proper education. For instance, he attended the Boston Grammar School for only one year because his parents could not afford the tuition. Later he spent a year at George Brownell's English School, where he failed arithmetic. Luckily, because Franklin's parents encouraged reading, thinking, and discussion, he grew up in an intellectual environment. He began working at the age of ten as an apprentice (one who learns by practical experience) in his father's chandlery shop (a place where candles are made).

Since Franklin enjoyed reading, his parents eventually decided he should enter the printing trade. Therefore, at the age of twelve, he became an apprentice for his brother James, who ran a Boston newspaper, *The New England Courant.* James's printing shop was a center of social activity, which provided Ben with a constant flow of new ideas. Customers would often linger to discuss politics or religion, and they also brought books for him to borrow. During this time the ambitious young man improved his writing and editing talents. At the age of seventeen Franklin left Boston to seek his fortune elsewhere.

Settles in Philadelphia

Franklin finally settled in Philadelphia in 1726. Three years later he purchased a failing newspaper, *The Pennsylvania Gazette,* and eventually made it one of the more popular papers in the colony. In 1733 he also began publishing *Poor Richard's Almanack,* a collection of witty sayings and pieces of advice that he wrote under the pseudonym (pen name) of Richard Saunders. During the 1730s Franklin branched out into other projects. In 1736 he founded the Union Fire Company in Philadelphia. The industrious young man also started a police force and promoted the paving and lighting of city streets. Inspired by his lifelong love of reading, Franklin founded what was probably the first circulating library in America. Established in 1731, it was originally a subscription library to which members contributed an annual fee in return for the full use of books and pamphlets. In 1736 Franklin was appointed clerk (official in charge of records) of the Pennsyl-

Poor Richard's Almanack

In 1733 Benjamin Franklin began publishing *Poor Richard's Almanack,* a collection of witty sayings and pieces of advice that he wrote under the pseudonym of Richard Saunders. The *Almanack* was an instant and enduring success, selling more than 10,000 copies annually. The book contained Franklin's own formula for success. Sayings such as "Haste makes Waste," "God helps them that help themselves," and "Eat to live, and not live to eat" provided a practical philosophy for English colonists who had to endure a difficult life. So popular were these sayings that they have a permanent place in American culture.

vania Assembly (legislative body), where he gained valuable political experience over the next fifteen years.

Begins electrical experiments

During the 1740s scientists around the world were investigating static (accumulated) electricity. Franklin first witnessed this new force in a demonstration of the Leyden jar (a device used for producing electrical energy) in 1743. The Leyden jar was simply a bottle filled with water that had a stopper in an opening on one end. Through the stopper was inserted a metal rod that extended into the water. A machine was used to create a static electric charge that was stored in the jar. Anyone who touched the end of the charged rod received an electrical jolt. Public demonstrations, in which many people joined hands and received a shock at the same time, were highly popular at the time.

Franklin was so inspired by the Leyden jar that he conducted his own experiments, thus beginning his career as an amateur scientist. Investigating the source of the electrical shock, he poured the charged water out of the jar into another bottle and discovered that the water no longer held a charge. Franklin suspected this result indicated that the glass itself had produced the shock. To verify his theory, Franklin took a window pane and placed a sheet of lead (a heavy, soft metal) on each side. He electrified the lead, removed each sheet, and then tested the lead for a charge. Neither sheet gave a single spark, but the window pane had been charged. Franklin had unknowingly invented the electrical condenser, which was named later by Italian physicist Alessandro Volta. The condenser is now used in radios, televisions, telephones, radar systems, and many other devices.

Through further experiments, Franklin discovered that electricity is an independent force, which he called "electrical fire." According to Franklin, a substance with a shortage of electrical fire has a negative, or minus, electrical charge. An element with extra electrical charge has a positive, or plus, electrical charge. He believed that electricity flows from plus to minus, but scientists now know that the opposite is true. Franklin also introduced the important concept known as conservation of charge. (Conservation of charge states that for every amount of charge gained by one body, an equal amount of charge must be lost by another body.) The idea that the overall electrical energy in a system does not increase or decrease is now a fundamental law in science. Franklin introduced many other terms that still pertain to electricity, including battery, conductor, charge, and discharge. He also discovered that electricity moves particularly well through metals and water.

Performs kite experiment

Drawing a parallel between the sparking and crackling of the charged Leyden jar and the lightning and thunder that occur during a storm, Franklin wondered if there was an electrical charge in the sky. To test his idea he devised the Philadelphia experiment, which he published in a book that was widely read in Europe. According to his plan for the experiment, he would erect a long metal rod atop Christ Church in Philadelphia. During a lightning storm the rod would conduct electricity to a sentry box (a guard station). A man standing on an insulated (protected) platform would then collect the electric charge. Since Franklin had already published his idea, however, he was not the first to conduct the experiment. On May 10, 1752, a French scientist named D'Alibard performed the test himself by charging a Leyden jar with lightning. Franklin recognized D'Alibard as being the pioneer, but Franklin did receive credit for inventing the lightning rod (a metallic rod with one end embedded in the ground, which diverts electricity to the Earth and protects buildings against fire caused by lightning). By 1782 there were four hundred lightning rods in Philadelphia.

While waiting for the lightning rod to be installed on Christ Church, Franklin came up with an idea for a faster way to get a conductor into the sky. He made a kite by tying a large silk handkerchief to two crossed wooden sticks. Next, he attached a long silk thread that had a metal key tied at the end of the kite. Then he waited for a thunderstorm. During the storm the rain soaked the thread, making it an excellent conductor (an item that permits flow of electric current) that transmitted a static charge from the sky down to the key. When Franklin touched his knuckle to the key, a spark jumped from the key to his hand, thus proving the existence of electricity in the sky. Franklin also stored the electric charge in a Leyden jar. Fortunately, Franklin had been wise enough to connect a ground wire to his key. (A ground wire diverts an electrical charge into the Earth.) Two other scientists attempted to duplicate the experiment but neglected to use the ground wire. They were struck by lightning and killed. Even with his precautions, however, Franklin was lucky not to have been hit by lightning himself.

Investigates other scientific areas

Although Franklin was best known for his work in electricity, he investigated other areas of science as well. His interest in the weather led him to notice that weather patterns usually travel from west to east. He suggested that this was due to the circulation of air masses (large accumulations), thus establishing the meteorological (having to do with weather) concepts of high and low pressure in the atmosphere. Another of Franklin's interests was the sea. During his diplomatic career he journeyed across the Atlantic Ocean eight times, and on these trips he took notes of his observations of ocean waters. With the help of a sea captain, he created the first chart of the Gulf Stream (a warm current in the Atlantic Ocean). Franklin also devised a method of using a thermometer to gauge water temperature to determine if a ship was on course in the Gulf Stream.

Franklin also introduced several innovations in the field of medicine. He was a strong supporter of regular exercise, particularly swimming. He believed in the importance of fresh air for good health, even though at the time many people thought night air and drafts caused disease. Expanding on his electrical studies, he used electric shocks to treat people with paralysis (loss of body movement). He determined, however, that the treatment did not have any permanent benefits. When smallpox inoculation was first introduced, Franklin warned against the practice. (Smallpox is a highly contagious, often fatal disease. Inoculation is the introduction of the disease-causing agent into the body in order to create an immunity.) After his own son died of the disease, however, he reversed his opinion and published a pamphlet on the importance of inoculation.

Makes international contributions

In 1748 Franklin retired from business and scientific study to devote the rest of his life to politics and diplomacy. Three years later he was elected to the Pennsylvania Assembly. In 1757 Franklin began his diplomatic career when he was sent to England as a lobbyist (one who represents a particular group in attempting to influence public officials). Franklin's experiments with electricity brought him great fame in America and Europe. Not only was he respected by the scientific community, he was popular with the general public. His ideas appeared in a number of writings, including articles in the leading scientific journal of the time, *Philosophical Transactions of the Royal Society.* In 1751 Franklin's papers on electricity were gathered and published in a ninety-page book in London. The Royal Society, a British scientific organization, awarded Franklin the Copley Medal in 1753 for his accomplishments and made him a member of the society in 1756. (In 1744 Franklin had modeled the American Philosophical Society on the prestigious Royal Society.)

Franklin received a number of honorary degrees from institutions such as Harvard University (1753), Yale University (1753), and Oxford University (1762). He was a member of the Second Continental Congress (the governing body of the Thirteen Colonies). In addition, he helped to draft the Declaration of Independence (a document that stated the American

 Invents practical devices

Benjamin Franklin was a great inventor who could turn ideas into practical, working items. One of his first major inventions was the Pennsylvania fireplace, now known as the Franklin stove, which he developed around 1740. Improving on an existing design, he equipped the stove with a flue (heat channel) that heats the air around it. The stove was highly efficient, and Franklin claimed it made a room twice as warm as other stoves even though it used only twenty-five percent of the usual amount of wood. Another popular Franklin invention was bifocal eyeglasses, in which the lower part of the lens is designed for near vision and the upper for distant vision. Franklin is also credited with creating the rocking chair.

colonists' reasons for demanding freedom from Great Britain), which was completed in 1776. Two years later he signed treaties with France that may have helped America win the Revolutionary War (1775–83; a conflict in which the American colonies won independence from Great Britain).

Twenty thousand attend funeral

During his lifetime, Franklin had a long union with Deborah Reed, whom he never married because she never officially divorced her husband. Franklin already had one son, William, born to an unknown mother, who joined his family. Franklin and Reed also had two children of their own, a son Francis (who died of smallpox) and a daughter Sarah. During the last few years of his life, Franklin lived with Sarah and numerous grandchildren in a large house on Market Street in Philadelphia. He spent his time completing his *Autobiography* (first published in 1868), which is a classic work in American literature. Franklin died in Philadelphia on April 17, 1790, at the age of eighty-five. His funeral was attended by approximately 20,000 people, who came to mourn the passing of a great man.

For further research

Benjamin Franklin: An Enlightened American, http://www.library.advanced. org/ 22254/home.htm Available July 13, 1999.

Benjamin Franklin Citizen of the World. A&E Home Video, 1994. Videocassette recording.

Benjamin Franklin Scientist and Inventor. Living History Productions, 1993. Videocassette recording.

Franklin, Benjamin. *Benjamin Franklin: A Biography in His Own Words.* Thomas Fleming, ed. New York: Newsweek, distributed by Harper & Row, 1972.

McFarland, Philip James. *The Brave Bostonians: Hutchinson, Quincy, Franklin, and The Coming of the American Revolution.* Boulder, Colorado: Westview Press, 1998.

Rudy, Lisa Jo, ed. *The Benjamin Franklin Book of Easy and Incredible Experiments.* New York: Wiley, 1995.

Marie Guyart

c. 1599
France
c. 1672
Quebec, France

French missionary

French missionary Marie Guyart was a pioneering educator in seventeenth-century Canada. Going against the wishes of her family, Guyart achieved her lifelong dream of becoming a nun (member of a Roman Catholic order for women). In 1631 she entered the Ursuline convent (a house where nuns live) in Tours, France, where she took the religious name Marie de l'Incarnation and began her spiritual training. Eight years later Guyart went to Canada and established a convent in New France (now Quebec). Her school for daughters of settlers and Native Americans thrived in spite of many hardships. A tireless missionary, Guyart also wrote instructional materials in Algonquian and Iroquoian. Her autobiography, titled *The Life of the Venerable Mother Marie de l'Incarnation* published in 1677, is an important document about the lives of Native American and European women in early Canada.

Pursues dream of becoming nun

Marie Guyart was born in France around 1599 to middle-class parents. Her father was a baker in the French textile center of Tours. As a young woman, Guyart had numerous

The Jesuits in Canada

French missionary and Roman Catholic nun Marie Guyart went to Canada in 1639 to work alongside the Jesuits, members of the Society of Jesus (a Roman Catholic religious order for men founded by St. Ignatius of Loyola). Jesuits are dedicated to academic study and the establishment of foreign missions and schools. Called the "Black Robes" (because of their clothing) by Native Americans, several Jesuits wrote accounts of their life in Canada. Among them was Jean de Brébeuf, whose narrative (dated 1635) reveals European attitudes toward Native Americans:

> Our Hurons, as you see, are not so dull as one might think them. They seem to me to have good common sense, and I find them universally very docile. Nevertheless, some of them are obstinate, and attached to their superstitions and evil customs. These are principally the old people; for beyond these, who are not numerous, the rest know nothing of their own belief. We have two or three of this number in our village. I am often in conflict with them; and then I show them they are wrong, and make them contradict themselves, so that they frankly admit their ignorance, and the others ridicule them; still they will not yield, always falling back upon this, that their country is not like ours, that they have another god, another paradise, in a word,

> other customs. . . . Two things among others have aided us very much in the little we have been able to do here, by the grace of our Lord; the first is, as I have already said, the good health that God has granted us in the midst of sickness so general and so widespread. [Possibly the Hurons were suffering from an epidemic disease brought by Europeans, who were immune and therefore did not become sick. Native Americans, on the other hand, had no built-in resistance and they died in great numbers.] For our Hurons have thought that if they believed in God and served them as we do, they would not die in so large numbers. The second is the temporal assistance we have rendered to the sick. . . . They seek baptism almost entirely as an aid to health. We try to purify this intention, and to lead them to receive from the hand of God alike sickness and health, death and life; and teach them that the life-giving waters of holy baptism principally impart life to the soul, and not to the body. However, they have the opinion so deeply rooted that the baptized, especially the children, are no longer sickly, that soon they will have spread it abroad and published it everywhere. The result is that they are now bringing us children to baptize from two, three, yes, even seven leagues away [a league equals 2.4 to 4.6 miles]. . . .

Reprinted in: Stiles, T. J., ed. In Their Own Words: The Colonizers. New York: Berkeley Publishing Group, 1998, p. 132.

mystical experiences and hoped to become a nun. Her father, who disapproved of her plans, arranged for her to be married to a silkmaker named Claude Martin. After they married in 1617, the couple had one son, Claude. Shortly before the child was a year old, Guyart's husband died.

After the death of her husband, Guyart refused to marry again. She and Claude took up residence in her sister's household. Guyart spent the next decade helping with her brother-in-law's carting (hauling) business by grooming horses, keeping books, and writing correspondence. Sometimes Guyart supervised all of the work. When she was not working, she was involved in religious activities. Her ultimate goal was to dedicate her life to God's service as a nun, even though that would mean leaving her son behind.

Establishes convent in Canada

Even though her family strongly discouraged her, Guyart never gave up her longing to be a nun. Finally her brother-in-law agreed to act as legal guardian for her son. He set aside a fund for Claude's upbringing in recognition of the fact that the family's recent prosperity owed much to Guyart's "talent for business." In January 1631 Guyart appeared at the door of the Ursuline Convent in Tours, France, and threw herself at the feet of the reverend mother (the nun who headed the convent). There she took the religious name Marie de l'Incarnation, and for the next few years she carried on a life of physical deprivation, constant devotion, and intensive spiritual training.

Guyart soon became an instructor of Christian doctrine in the convent, even writing explanations of the faith and a commentary on the Old Testament Song of Solomon. She also listened to the preaching of Jesuit fathers, some of whom had been missionaries in Canada and had returned with stories of people who had "knowledge of Jesus Christ." Eventually Guyart had a vision in which God told her to go to Canada and "make a house for Jesus and Mary [Jesus of Nazareth, the founder of Christianity, and his mother, the Virgin Mary]."

On May 4, 1639, Guyart went to Canada with the noble-born Madeleine de La Peltrie, who had pledged to devote her wealth and life to missionary work "in the service of savage girls." When they arrived in Quebec in August, Guyart kissed the soil on which she would spend the remainder of her life. Her work included establishing a convent, painting altars (a table or other structure used in worship services), cooking, lugging logs for building, studying Native American languages, and educating young Huron and Iroquois girls. Despite hardships, including threats from Native

The mission of San Diego de Alcala. It is similar to the mission where Guyart spent the remainder of her life in service.
Reproduced by permission of The Granger Collection.

Americans, the nuns remained in Canada and their convent flourished. Guyart served as the convent's mother superior for eighteen years and held other offices.

Writes spiritual autobiography

Through her writings, Guyart became a tireless promoter of the new convent in Quebec. She carried on an extensive correspondence with her family, friends, religious officials, and potential donors in France. Guyart composed accounts of her mission work for the *Jesuit Relations,* a popular collection of missionary narratives published annually in France to promote the Jesuits' work in Canada. In 1661 she began writing catechisms (a summary of religious doctrine often in the form of questions and answers), prayers, and instructional materials in the Algonquian and Iroquoian languages. Her best-known work, *Sacred History,* was a "big book of sacred history and holy things" written in Algonquian. Guyart died in Quebec in 1672.

Seven years before her death, Guyart wrote a spiritual autobiography at the request of her son. Although she had instructed him to keep it private, he published her autobiography as *La Vie de la venerable Mere Marie de l'Incarnation (The Life of the Venerable Mother Marie de l'Incarnation)* in 1677. Guyart's spiritual reflections and detailed accounts of mission life among Native Americans made the book a popular seller, spreading her fame throughout France. The autobiography remains an important source of information on how contact between the two races changed the lives of Native American and European women in seventeenth-century Canada.

For further research
Davis, Natalie Zemon. *Women on the Margins: Three Seventeenth-Century Lives.* Cambridge, Mass.: Harvard University Press, 1995.

Sigerman, Harriet, ed. *Young Oxford History of Women in the United States: Biographical Supplement and Index.* New York: Oxford University Press, 1994, pp. 71–72.

Stiles, T. J., ed. *In Their Own Words: The Colonizers.* New York: Berkeley Publishing Group, 1998, p. 132.

Henry Hudson

September 12, 1575
England
Disappeared 1611
Atlantic Ocean

English navigator and explorer

"[The chiefs] concluded it [the *Half Moon*] to be a large canoe or house, in which the great Mannitto (great or Supreme Being) himself was, and that he was probably coming to visit them."

Translation of traditional Delaware story by John Heckewelder.

Henry Hudson was an English explorer whose career was marked by both success and failure. Although he never managed to find either the Northeast Passage or the Northwest Passage to China, he did explore what came to be known as the Hudson River and the Hudson Bay (in present-day New York). His exploration of the Hudson River in 1609 led to the formation of the Dutch West India Company, a group which founded the colony of New Netherland (later New York) in 1624. During a second attempt to find the Northwest Passage in 1610, Hudson became the first explorer to sail through the Hudson Strait. During the following summer of 1611, Hudson's crew mutinied (staged a revolt) and he was set adrift in a small boat and never seen again.

Attempts to find passage to China

Nothing is known about the early life and career of Henry Hudson. He undertook his first recorded voyage in 1607, when he was hired by the Muscovy Company of England to search for the Northeast Passage, a sea route that led around the northern coast of Siberia to China. Hudson explored the coast of the Svalbard Islands in the Arctic Ocean and sighted Jan Mayen Island east of Greenland, but he did not find a sea passage to China. In 1608 he departed on another expedition to find the Northeast Passage. When his ship encountered heavy ice, however, he was forced to turn back without making any new discoveries.

In 1609 Hudson was hired by the Dutch East India Company to look for the Northeast Passage once again. He set out from the Netherlands on the ship *Half Moon* with a mixed crew of English and Dutch sailors. Beyond the North Cape, located off the northern coast of Norway in the Arctic Ocean, the ship ran into heavy ice, and Hudson's crew refused to go any farther. Instead of giving up again and returning to the Netherlands, however, Hudson decided to try to find the Northwest Passage, a water route between the Atlantic and Pacific Oceans. He turned the *Half Moon* west, heading for the coast of North America. His friend **John Smith** (see entry), the English explorer who had colonized Virginia, may have given Hudson this idea when he reportedly mentioned a large bay that might lead to a Northwest Passage.

Explores Hudson River

Hudson and his crew reached the coast of Nova Scotia (a province on the east coast of Canada) in July 1609, traveling as far as Chesapeake Bay before turning north to explore Delaware Bay. Continuing north, Hudson and his crew reached Sandy Hook, a peninsula at the entrance to New York Harbor, on September 12, 1609. The Italian explorer **Giovanni da Verrazano** (see entry) had already discovered the entrance to the harbor in 1524 but had not been able to explore farther inland. Hudson sailed up the wide river that now bears his name to the site of present-day Albany, New York. Some of his crew members then rowed a boat even farther north.

During his voyage up and down the river, Hudson noted the richness of the land and recognized the opportunity for a prosperous fur trade. His favorable report inspired the Dutch to form a new company, the Dutch West India Company, which founded the colony of New Netherland along the Hudson and Delaware Rivers in 1614. Hudson and his party did have a few unfriendly encounters with Native Americans along the way. During a particularly violent skirmish, one of

Henry Hudson (standing in canoe, holding hat) with members of his crew and some Native Americans they encountered during his voyage along the Hudson River.
Reproduced by permission of the Library of Congress.

his crew members was killed by an arrow through the throat. Relations improved, however, when Hudson traded European goods for food. Before heading back across the Atlantic, the *Half Moon* stayed for several days in New York Harbor on what Hudson described as "that side of the river that is called Manna-hatta"—a Native American word for the island now called Manhattan.

Voyage to Hudson Bay

On the return voyage to Europe, the *Half Moon* stopped in the English port of Dartmouth on November 7, 1609. Because the Dutch had financed Hudson's expedition, the British authorities took him and other English crew members off the ship, forbidding them to work for a foreign country again. Hudson would not be discouraged, however, and he soon convinced a group of English investors to support a journey to renew the search for the Northwest Passage. This time

Hudson encounters Delaware

While exploring the Hudson and Delaware Rivers in present-day New York, Henry Hudson and his party encountered a Native American group, the Delawares. This was the first time the Delawares had seen Europeans, so the experience was quite unsettling for them. Following are excerpts from a Delaware tribe account of sighting Hudson's ship, the *Half Moon*, which was anchored off the coast of Manhattan Island. The story was written down in the eighteenth century by John Heckewelder, an English missionary who interviewed descendants of the Delawares.

A long time ago, when there was no such thing known to the Indians as people with white skin [their expression], some Indians who had been out fishing, and where the sea widens, espied [caught sight of] at a great distance something remarkably large swimming, or floating on the water, and such as they had never seen before. They immediately returning to the shore, appraised their countrymen of what they had seen, and pressed them to go out with them and discover what it might be . . . . [Some concluded] it either to be an uncommon large fish, or other animal, while others were of the opinion it must be some very large house. . . . [Finally] they sent runners and watermen off to carry the news to their scattered chiefs . . . . [The chiefs] arriving in numbers, and themselves viewing the strange appearance . . . concluded it to be a large canoe or house, in which the great Mannitto (great or Supreme Being) himself was, and that he was probably coming to visit them. By this time the chiefs of the different tribes were assembled on York island, and were counselling (or deliberating) on the manner they should receive their Mannitto on his arrival. Every step had been taken to be well provided with plenty of meat for a sacrifice; the women were required to prepare the best victuals [food]; idols or images were examined and put in order; and a grand dance was supposed not only to be an agreeable entertainment for the Mannitto, but it might, with the addition of sacrifice, contribute toward appeasing him, in case he was angry with them. . . . Between hope and fear, and in confusion a dance commenced. While in this situation fresh runners arrive declaring it a house of various colours, crowded with living creatures . . . ; but other runners soon after arriving, declare it a large house of various colours, full of people of a different colour than they [the Native Americans] are of; that they are also dressed in a different manner from them, and one in particular appeared altogether red, which must be the Mannitto himself. . . . Many are for running off into the woods, but are pressed to stay, in order not to give offense to their visitors.

Reprinted in: Middleton, Richard. Colonial America: A History, 1585–1776, second edition. Malden, Mass.: Blackwell, 1996, pp. 30–31.

he planned to explore farther north than on his previous voyage. Hudson set sail for North America on April 17, 1610, on the ship *Discovery*. Almost immediately there were signs of trouble among his crew, whom Hudson apparently could not control. Nonetheless, they reached North America, and in

June they sighted Resolution Island, which separates Davis Strait from what is now called Hudson Strait in northeastern Canada. The strait had already been discovered by the English navigator Martin Frobisher, in 1578, but Hudson was the first to sail through it. The voyage took six weeks.

Hudson and his crew then rounded Cape Wolstenholme, named after one of the financial backers of the voyage, and entered Hudson Bay. At this point Hudson believed he had sailed from the Atlantic to the Pacific. He soon recognized, however, that he was mistaken. When the *Discovery* turned south into what is now known as James Bay, the southern extension of Hudson Bay, he found that they were landlocked (almost completely surrounded by land). By this time it was October and the bay was beginning to freeze, so the Englishmen were forced to spend the entire winter stuck in the ice. Because of Hudson's lack of foresight, he and his crew did not have enough food and other necessities for the winter. Although they had made contact with nearby Native Americans, efforts at trading with them had failed. Everyone aboard the *Discovery* suffered from the extremely harsh weather and lack of supplies, and there was frequent fighting among the crew members.

Set adrift on Atlantic

On June 12, 1611, the ice had melted enough for the *Discovery* to begin its voyage home to England. When the ship reached Charlton Island in the southern part of James Bay on June 23, the crew mutinied against Hudson. The following morning they put Hudson, his nineteen-year-old son, and six of the weaker crew members on a small boat and set them adrift. Hudson and his party were never seen or heard from again.

Now captained by Robert Bylot, the *Discovery* continued north through Hudson Bay and anchored at Digges Island at the entrance to Hudson Bay. During a battle with a party of Inuit (Eskimo), the ringleader of the mutiny, Henry Greene, and several other crewmen were killed. The survivors escaped and finally landed in southern Ireland, where the crew was rescued and taken to London, England. Only eight men survived the voyage back across the Atlantic. No one was ever convicted of any charges connected with the mutiny or with the banishment of Hudson, his son, and the other crew members.

For further research

Henry Hudson and the Half Moon. http://www.ulster.net/_hrmm/half-moon/halfmoon.htm Available July 13, 1999.

The Life and Times of Henry Hudson, explorer and adventurer. http://www.georgian.net/rally/hudson/ Available July 13, 1999.

Middleton, Richard. *Colonial America: A History, 1585–1776,* second edition. Malden, Mass.: Blackwell, 1996, pp. 30–31.

Rachlis, Eugene. *The Voyages of Henry Hudson.* New York: Random House, 1962.

Syme, Ronald. *Henry Hudson.* New York: Morrow, 1955. (Fiction)

Weiner, Eric. *The Story of Henry Hudson, Master Explorer.* New York: Dell, 1991.

Anne Marbury Hutchinson

1591
Alford, Lincolnshire, England
c. 1643
Pelham Bay Park, New York

Religious leader

A nne Marbury Hutchinson was a religious rebel whose ideas threatened the rule of the Puritan government in the Massachusetts Bay Colony. (The Puritans were a religious group who believed in strict moral and spiritual codes.) Born in England, she received a strong religious education as a young woman and was later influenced by the Puritan preachings of **John Cotton** (see entry). She was particularly inspired by Cotton's concept of the Covenant of Grace (see below). After emigrating (moving from one country to another) to Boston in 1634, Hutchinson began to preach her own extreme version of the Covenant of Grace during private meetings with other Puritans. Eventually her following grew, creating a division in the colony that had social as well as religious repercussions. By the time Hutchinson went to trial for heresy (violation of accepted religious beliefs or doctrines) in 1638 she had already made a major impact on colonial American history.

Influenced by her father

Anne Hutchinson was born in Alford, Lincolnshire, England, in 1591. She was baptized into the Anglican faith

Portrait: Anne Hutchinson.
Reproduced by permission of Corbis-Bettmann.

144

(the official religion of England, also known as the Church of England). Her father, Anglican clergyman Francis Marbury, was imprisoned twice for rejecting church dogma (established opinion). After his second imprisonment, Marbury moved to Alford and married Bridget Dryden. Of their thirteen children, Hutchinson was the eldest daughter. Raised in a religious household, she received an education far superior to that provided to most young women of the time. She participated in religious discussions and she became familiar with church doctrine and scripture (passages from the Bible). Hutchinson was also heavily influenced by her father's rebellious spirit and his contempt for authority.

In 1605 the family moved to London, England. In 1612 Anne married William Hutchinson, an affluent businessman. Throughout their marriage, William was a devoted husband who always supported his wife's religious beliefs. After their marriage, the Hutchinsons moved to Alford, where they lived for the next twenty-two years. While living in Alford, Anne attended services at Cotton's church, St. Botolph's in Boston, Lincolnshire. Between 1613 and 1630 Hutchinson gave birth to twelve children. Three of those children died and, beginning in 1631, she had three more. Her last child was born in 1636, after the family had moved to the Massachusetts Bay Colony.

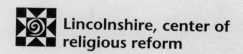

Lincolnshire, center of religious reform

While living in Alford, Lincolnshire, England, Anne Hutchinson was consumed by the thriving religious environment. At the time Lincolnshire was a center for Puritans and other reforming Anglicans who challenged the dogma of traditional churches. Thus laymen who felt they had received grace gathered together informally to discuss sermons, debate passages of scripture, and pray without the presence of ordained ministers. Women played a particularly active role in these assemblies. Hutchinson took this opportunity to hone her natural intellect and leadership skills.

Inspired by Covenant of Grace

At the time Hutchinson began attending St. Botolph's Church, Cotton was attempting to modify Puritan doctrine. One of the central doctrines of Puritanism was the belief that salvation could be earned only through good works, such as self-sacrifice, charity, and moral behavior. This was known to many as the Covenant of Works. Hutchinson was inspired by

Cotton's emphasis upon the Covenant of Grace rather than the Covenant of Works. According to the Covenant of Grace, a Christian believer could gain salvation (be saved from sins) through direct communication with God. This doctrine became popular because it freed people from performing good works in order to earn salvation. Cotton insisted, however, that his followers continue doing good works. Although Hutchinson believed in the Covenant of Grace, she took the idea much further than Cotton intended.

Hutchinson believed that individuals who had achieved grace were the actual embodiment of the spirit of God. Therefore, according to Hutchinson, the Covenant of Grace made the Covenant of Works unnecessary. If individuals had this special connection with God, then good works were not required to gain salvation. The problem with Hutchinson's theory was that it verged upon Antimonian heresy (the belief that faith alone is enough to gain salvation), which stated that Christians were free from the moral obligations of the Old Testament (a part of the Bible). Puritan leaders feared that if the Covenant of Works became obsolete, then the power of religious officials would become obsolete as well, since they decided who was saved or not. Hutchinson's adherence to the Covenant of Grace can be attributed to the death of two of her daughters in 1630 and the later death of her father. She claimed to have received divine revelation from God stating that she was saved from sin during these experiences.

Holds controversial meetings

Because of his nonconformist views, Cotton was forced out of his ministry in England in 1633. He then fled to the Massachusetts Bay Colony and took a position at the Puritan church in Boston. After Cotton was gone, Hutchinson announced to her family that God had instructed her to follow him. A year later the Hutchinsons left England on board the *Griffin*. In September 1634 they arrived in Boston, where William Hutchinson entered into the textile trade. His eventual success propelled the Hutchinson family into a prominent position in the community. Anne Hutchinson's kind manner and skills as a midwife (a person who assists women during childbirth) made her popular with affluent Boston women.

Anne Hutchinson preaching in her Boston home during one of her private meetings. *Reproduced by permission of the Library of Congress.*

confusing tenets (principles or doctrines) of Puritanism. Finally, her religious fervor would take over, and she often became careless in presenting her own ideas and labeling them as Cotton's. The meetings became quite popular among wealthy Bostonians. Before long, Hutchinson had many followers who believed in her version, rather than Cotton's, of the Covenant of Grace.

Hutchinson conducted her meetings without interruption until 1635, when the prominent Puritan clergyman John Wilson returned to Boston from England. Hutchinson did not agree with Wilson's sermons, so she informed her followers that he was simply preaching another version of the Covenant of Works. Then she announced that most Massachusetts clergymen were promoting this doctrine. The only exceptions, she said, were Cotton and her brother-in-law, John Wheelwright, both of whom preached the Covenant of Grace. Soon Hutchinson had created a division between her followers and traditional Puritans. The rift rapidly spread through the entire colony, becoming a serious threat to the survival of the settlement in 1637, when her male followers refused to fight in the Pequot War. (The Pequot War broke out when the Puritans, in retaliation for the murder of two English traders by Native Americans, nearly exterminated the Pequot tribe.) Alarmed at her growing power, Puritan officials immediately charged Hutchinson with heresy.

Tried for heresy

Although Hutchinson was the principal agitator in the Puritan conflict, she was not the first to be punished. In March 1637 Wheelwright was brought before the General Court and charged with sedition (resistance against lawful authority). It was not until September 1637 that a church synod (advisory council) finally condemned Hutchinson for her religious beliefs. By this time, she had lost much of her support. For instance, after **John Winthrop** (see entry) was elected governor of the Massachusetts Bay Colony, several of Hutchinson's followers were removed from public office. Furthermore, Cotton was unwilling to sacrifice his religious beliefs and his power in the colony and sided with the church instead of Hutchinson. Wheelwright, her only remaining ally, was banished from (required to leave) the colony in November 1637.

After Wheelwright was banished, Hutchinson was brought before the General Court and accused of "traducing [exposing to shame or blame by means of falsehood and misrepresentation] the ministers and their ministry." The judge read the charges: "You are called hither as one of those who have had a great share in the causes of our public disturbances, partly by those erroneous opinions which you have broached and divulged amongst us, and maintaining them, partly by countenancing and encouraging such as have sowed seditions amongst us, partly by casting reproach upon the faithful." She was further accused of undermining the "Ministers of this Country . . . and so weakening their hands in the work of the Lord, and raising prejudice against them, in the hearts of their people, and partly by maintaining weekly and public meetings in your house, to the offence of all the Country, and the detriment of many families, and still upholding the same, since such meetings were clearly condemned in the late general Assembly." Hutchinson was also charged with violating laws that forbade her, as a woman, to teach men or people older than herself and prohibited her from speaking in public. She countered each of these accusations, stating that she did not have to answer to the court, only to God.

Banned from colony

At one point during the trial, Hutchinson was nearly cleared of all charges. Then she announced that she had received a direct revelation from God. This was clearly a heretical claim because Puritan leaders believed that God spoke to humans only through the Bible. The frightened judges immediately ruled that Hutchinson was to be banished from the colony. She would be allowed to remain through the winter, but she was to be placed in the custody of deputy Joseph Weld of Roxbury. Despite Weld's attempts to persuade her to renounce her rebellious views, Hutchinson continued to speak out against the church.

When Hutchinson was brought to trial again in March 1638, she failed to convince the judges that she had genuinely repented (expressed regret for her behavior). She

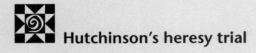

Hutchinson's heresy trial

In 1637 and 1638 Anne Hutchinson was tried for heresy by the General Court of the Massachusetts Bay Colony, which accused her of "traducing the [Puritan] ministers and their ministry." Ultimately found guilty, she was excommunicated from the Congregationalist (Puritan) Church and banished from the colony. Following is an excerpt from the trial, in which Hutchinson defended herself against charges of violating laws that prohibited her from holding public meetings:

Court: " . . . what say you to your weekly public meetings? can you show a warrant for them?"

Hutchinson: "I will show you how I took it up, there were such meetings in use before I came, and because I went to none of them, this was the special reason of my taking up this course, we began it but with five or six, and though it grew to more in future time, yet being tolerated at the first, I knew not why it might not continue."

Court: "There were private meetings indeed, and are still in many places, of some few neighbours, but not so public and frequent as yours, and are of use for increase of love, and mutual edification, but yours are of another nature, if they had been such as yours they had been evil, and therefore no good warrant to justify yours; but answer by what authority, or rule, you uphold them."

was therefore formally excommunicated (excluded her from the rights of the church) from the Congregational (Puritan) Church. Hutchinson left Massachusetts with her family and moved to a settlement on the island of Aquidneck in Narragansett Bay. She was followed by more than eighty families of supporters who had also been excommunicated for believing in Hutchinson's views. Among them was Quaker dissenter (a religious nonconformist) **Mary Dyer** (see entry), who was executed for heresy in Boston two decades later. After William Hutchinson died in 1642, Anne Hutchinson moved with her six youngest children to the Dutch colony of New Netherland (now New York). They settled in Pelham Bay Park (now the Bronx section of New York City, near the Hutchinson River, which was named for Anne Hutchinson). The following year Hutchinson and five of her children were attacked and killed by Native Americans.

Hutchinson: " . . . where the elder women are to teach the younger."

Court: "So we allow you to do . . . privately, and upon occasion, but that gives no warrant of such set meetings for that purpose; and besides, you take upon you to teach many that are elder than yourself, neither do you teach them that which the Apostle commands [namely] to keep at home."

Hutchinson: "Will you please to give me a rule against it, and I will yield?"

Court: "You must have a rule for it, or else you cannot do it in faith, yet you have a plain rule against it; I permit not a woman to teach."

Hutchinson: "That is meant of teaching men."

Court: "If a man in distress of conscience or other temptation, &c. should come and ask your counsel in private, might you not teach him?"

Hutchinson: "Yes."

Court: "Then it is clear, that it is not meant of teaching men, but of teaching in public."

Hutchinson: "It is said, I will pour my Spirit upon your Daughters, and they shall prophesier &c. If God give me a gift of Prophecy, I may use it."

Reprinted in: Kupperman, Karen Ordahl, ed. Major Problems in American Colonial History. *Lexington, MA: D. C. Heath and Company, 1993, pp. 159–62.*

Movement has lasting impact

Hutchinson was banished from the Massachusetts Bay Colony for reasons other than purely religious. Her accusers were also concerned about the impact of her teachings on the social structure of the colony. By adhering to the Covenant of Grace, Hutchinson taught that individuals could act as they chose because they had already received the grace of God. But the Massachusetts colony was founded on the Covenant of Works, and Puritan leaders were always striving to become more pious (virtuous). By attracting believers to the Covenant of Grace, Hutchinson thus undermined the very foundation of the colony. Many leaders feared her teachings would lessen their power over citizens. Her accusers labeled her an anarchist (one who rebels against any authority) and some even thought she was a witch (one who is thought to have supernatural powers). Many historians contend that she was not an advocate of religious freedom because she did not tolerate other views. The movement inspired by Hutchinson, however, left an indelible mark on colonial American history.

For further research

Crawford, Deborah. *Four Women in a Violent Time: Anne Hutchinson (1591–1643), Mary Dyer (1591?–1660), Lady Deborah Moody (1660–1659), Penelope Stout (1622–1732).* New York: Crown Publishers, 1970.

Faber, Doris. *Anne Hutchinson.* Champaign, IL: Garrard Publishing Co., 1970.

Kupperman, Karen Ordahl, ed. *Major Problems in American Colonial History.* Lexington, MA: D. C. Heath and Company, 1993, pp. 159–62.

Williams, Selma R. *Divine Rebel: The Life of Anne Marbury Hutchinson.* New York: Holt, Rinehart, and Winston, 1981.

Anthony Johnson

Not known
Not known
After 1665
Somerset County, Maryland

Freedman and landowner

The life of Anthony Johnson, an African American landowner in colonial Virginia, presents an intriguing story. At a time when few former slaves could own property, Johnson amassed a sizable estate. He was brought to North America in 1621 and worked as a slave on a Virginia plantation. Gaining his freedom around 1635, he began acquiring his own plantation little by little during the 1640s. By 1651 he owned two hundred and fifty acres of land. Even a catastrophic fire that destroyed much of his estate in 1653 could not halt Johnson's rise to success. Historians believe that Johnson was immensely talented and energetic, enabling him to become what they call the "black patriarch" of Pungoteague Creek (the area of Virginia where his estate was located).

Works as plantation slave

Anthony Johnson arrived aboard the *James* in Virginia in 1621, two years after African slaves were first brought to the colony. Initially he was called "Antonio the negro," and there is no indication of how he acquired the surname Johnson (scholars speculate that a white man named Johnson may

> " . . . but now I know myne owne ground and I will worke when I please and play when I please."
>
> *Anthony Johnson*

Was Johnson unique?

Historical records show that Anthony Johnson, a freed slave, became a wealthy landowner in colonial Virginia. Yet historians have different ideas about how to interpret his success. They ask: Did other former slaves own large estates? Or was Johnson unique? Scholars did not seriously investigate the history of Virginia until the early twentieth century. By then, they tended to undervalue the significance of African American citizens such as Johnson. For instance, in *Economic History of Virginia in the Seventeenth Century* (1907), historian Philip Alexander Bruce commented that Johnson was only one of "a number of persons of African blood in the Colony, who had raised themselves to a condition of moderate importance in the community." John H. Russell, the author of *The Free Negro in Virginia 1619–1865* (1913), offered a more thorough account of Johnson's life. After comparing Johnson to his contemporaries, however, Russell still considered his success unusual but not especially remarkable.

have helped Anthony gain his freedom). Nothing is known about his earlier life. At that time, many Africans were indentured servants (people who worked for a specific period of time in order to buy their freedom). Black indentured servitude was prevalent in all colonies, but especially in the North. This was generally the case up to the 1760s, when most Africans remained in bondage for the rest of their lives. Prior to this time, however, some Africans who were indentured servants, and even some slaves were able to gain their freedom. In 1760 there were two thousand freed slaves (two to three percent of the African American population) in Virginia, and in the North about ten percent of the total African American population were freedmen (in Connecticut over twenty percent). Johnson, however, was a slave (a worker who was owned by a plantation owner and had to petition for freedom), and records show that he was purchased to work in the tobacco fields of the Warresquioake plantation, which was located on the James River. Warresquioake was owned by Edward Bennett, a wealthy Englishman who was participating in a program launched by the Virginia Company of London, England. The goal of the program was to make large sums of money in the New World (a European term for North America and South America) by using white and black indentured servants and slaves to cultivate crops such as tobacco. The English had found that buying tobacco from Spain was too expensive, so great hopes were placed in meeting the high demand for tobacco by producing it in English-owned American colonies. The project was led by Edwin Sandys, who favored Bennett and enabled him to purchase an estate that generated especially good profits. Warresquioake was run by Bennett's brother, Robert, and his nephew Richard, who at one time owned or employed more than sixty workers.

Survives Native American attack

Life in the Virginia colony was extremely difficult and even dangerous for slaves and servants, most of whom were teenagers and young men. Required to perform grueling labor in isolated fields, they were provided few comforts. Often these men met early and violent deaths because there was little security from attacks by the neighboring Tidewater tribe, Native Americans who were generally hostile to colonists. Johnson's own experience, which took place a year or so after he arrived at Warresquioake, illustrates the hazards of plantation life. On the morning of March 22, 1622, he was working in the fields when Native Americans launched a preplanned attack and massacred more than three hundred colonists in the area. They killed fifty-two people at Warresquioake, but Johnson was fortunately among the four survivors. By 1625 only twelve servants remained at Warresquioake, which had been renamed Bennett's Welcome.

On an unknown date shortly after the attack, Johnson was married to an African woman named Mary. She had arrived in Virginia in 1622 aboard the *Margrett and John*. Three years later she was the only woman living at Warresquioake. The unequal ratio of women to men was common at the time, since most employers, especially plantation owners, preferred male indentured servants and slaves for doing heavy labor. Women servants and slaves were used primarily for household work (though women slaves sometimes worked in the fields), and this kind of help was considered an unnecessary luxury that few people could afford. Therefore, most servants and slaves were men. As a result, male slaves and servants, white or black, led very lonely lives because they had few chances of

Africans in America

In 1998 the Public Broadcasting System (PBS) television network produced *Africans in America,* a four-part, six-hour program on the African American experience. The series traces the history of African Americans from their arrival in Virginia in 1619 through the late twentieth century. Anthony Johnson is mentioned in the first segment. *Africans in America* is available on videocassette. A companion book by the same title was also published.

A Virginia planter and his clerk overseeing slaves, who like Johnson, pack dried tobacco leaves for shipment to England. *Reproduced by permission of The Granger Collection.*

ever marrying and raising a family. Historians consider Johnson lucky to have found a wife. The Johnsons had four children, and over the years the extended family became quite prosperous.

"I know myne owne grounde"

Although little is known about Johnson's life between 1625 and 1650, records show that he and Mary gained their freedom before 1635. They moved to Northampton County, Virginia, with their former master, Richard Bennett. After Bennett became governor of Virginia, he helped the Johnsons with legal and economic matters. As a freedman (former servants and slaves), Johnson was granted land as part of his "freedom dues" (items given when to freedmen when they were released from servitude). As a result, Johnson acquired land during the 1640s and began raising livestock. T. H. Breen and Stephen Innes, in *Myne Owne Ground* (1980), note that a case involving

"Anthony the negro" and a Captain Philip Taylor is mentioned in Northampton County court records for 1645. According to a report given by Edwyn Conaway, the clerk of courts, Anthony and Taylor were both interested in owning a particular cornfield. One day Anthony and Taylor went out to the field to discuss the matter. When they returned, Conaway asked Anthony what they had decided. Conaway quoted Anthony as saying, "Mr. Taylor and I have devided our Corne And I am very glad of it [for] now I know myne owne, hee finds fault with mee that I doe not worke, but now I know myne owne ground and I will worke when I please and play when I please."

By 1651 Johnson owned 250 acres along Pungoteague Creek, which was considered a sizable estate at the time. On his plantation he used slaves and indentured servants as workers. Many white colonists could not afford to own any land at the time, so the fact that Johnson acquired considerable holdings is particularly unusual. Even more remarkably, he ultimately enjoyed a social status fairly close to that of white planters. Tragedy struck in February 1653, however, when much of Johnson's estate was destroyed by fire. This disastrous event set off a series of court cases that tested Johnson and his position as a landowner.

Position supported by courts

The first time Johnson appeared before the Northampton courts, he petitioned for tax exemption (at the time, taxes were levied on people, not land or livestock). The court responded by excusing his wife Mary and their two daughters from paying taxes. This action not only enabled Johnson to recover his losses but also made the Johnson women equal to the wives of white planters in Northampton County. White women did not pay taxes because they were engaged only in domestic work. In addition, physical labor was considered demeaning to a well-bred woman.

Johnson had similar results when he appeared before the court again on October 8, 1653. This time he was involved in a dispute over livestock with Lieutenant John Neale, who belonged to a powerful, white Virginia family. During the case, an investigation into the charges was led by Samuel Gouldsmith and Robert Parker, farmers who were familiar with business practices in the Pungoteague region. In spite of Neale's social status, the court once again ruled in favor of Johnson. While documents provide few details, historians assume that the outcome is further testimony to Johnson's high standing in the community. It also reveals concessions granted by Gouldsmith and Parker, who evidently believed that Johnson needed assistance after the fire on his estate.

Involved in slave ownership dispute

A year after the second court case, Johnson was embroiled in controversy one more time. Gouldsmith was paying a visit to the Johnson plantation when he was approached by John Casor, one of the workers. Pleading with Gouldsmith, Casor claimed that he was an indentured servant, not a slave, and that he had been held on the Johnson plantation illegally for seven years. After Johnson said he was not aware that Casor was indentured, Parker stepped in and took Casor to his farm. Parker claimed that Casor was indentured to a man named Mr. Sandys and that he was a runaway. Parker needed more field hands, so he apparently invented this story and took the opportunity to recruit an able-bodied worker. After deciding to set Casor free, Johnson changed his mind and asked the court to punish Parker for his conduct. On March 8, 1655, the court ruled that Parker had acquired Casor illegally and that Casor should be returned to Johnson.

This case is both culturally and historically significant. All of the participants had different perspectives about the social structure of Northampton County and their position within it. Therefore much of the tension arose from each person's sense of his own status in the community. Johnson saw that his own power lay in the fact that he was in agreement with white authorities on the issue of property ownership. Significantly, Johnson's values as a black owner of black slaves coincided with those held by the white aristocracy (a small privileged social class). Historians note, however, that at no time did anyone question whether or not slavery was wrong.

Johnsons are respected landowners

Although it is not clear why Johnson was granted so many favorable decisions by the Northampton courts, evidence suggests that he was considered a respected member of

A story of early black identity?

T. H. Breen and Stephen Innes have pieced together whatever facts remain about the Johnson family in the first chapter of *"Myne Owne Ground": Race and Freedom on Virginia's Eastern Shore, 1640–1676* (1980). In the preface to the book they note that Anthony Johnson "more than held his own, and the story of the Pungoteague patriarch and his sons becomes an early chapter in the saga of Old World immigrants 'making it' in America." Yet Breen and Innes are intrigued about the full meaning of the story. The authors point out that even though the Johnsons had assimilated into white society in colonial Virginia, they held themselves apart: "If the Johnsons were merely English colonists with black skins, then why did John, junior [Anthony's grandson], name his small farm 'Angola'? His action, admittedly a small shred of evidence, suggests the existence of a deeply rooted separate culture."

Breen and Innes go on to note that the family "was composed entirely of black men and women, and while one might argue that the Johnsons were constrained by external forces to marry people of their own race, they appear in their most intimate relations to have maintained a conscious black identity." The authors conclude that such an identity appeared to have been possible for African Americans, who were a small minority of the population in the mid-1600s. Families like the Johnsons were able to find their place alongside other struggling immigrant groups. But by 1705, the Johnsons disappear from public records. Breen and Innes speculate that Anthony Johnson's descendants may have lost their freedom or moved to the North, where slavery was illegal. By that time institutionalized slavery was in full force, and African Americans had no role in southern society except as slaves.

the community. Historians point out that in 1650 opportunities were available to African Americans—for instance, they could buy their freedom and own land. By the early eighteenth century, however, all Africans in the South were slaves and therefore had no chance of acquiring freedom or owning property. Whatever the reasons for Johnson's affluence and standing in the community, he managed to build a large estate and he and his wife raised equally successful children.

By 1652 the Johnsons' son John had acquired 450 acres of land, and in 1654 their son Richard owned 100 acres.

Both sons married and had their own families. While they all lived on separate estates, the Johnsons worked together and collaborated on legal and economic matters. Although Mary, John, and Richard had a voice in making decisions, Anthony was head of the family. Around 1665, when many planters were leaving Virginia in search of better land, the entire Johnson family moved to Somerset County, Maryland. They leased a 300-acre plantation, which they called "Tonies Vineyard." Johnson died soon afterwards. John Johnson took his father's position as head of the estate, eventually achieving the status of "planter." (As the owner of a plantation, a planter held considerable power and gained great respect in the southern colonies.) Mary outlived her husband by several years. In 1677 John Johnson's son, John Jr., acquired a forty-acre farm that he named "Angola," perhaps after the African country. Around the turn of the eighteenth century, however, the Johnsons seemed to disappear. Public records do not show any evidence of their existence in Maryland or elsewhere. The end of the Anthony Johnson story, like the beginning, is open to speculation.

For further research

Breen, T. H. and Stephen Innes. *"Myne Owne Ground": Race and Freedom on Virginia's Eastern Shore, 1640–1676.* New York: Oxford University Press, 1980.

Introduction to Slavery. http://www.coe.ufl.edu/course/edtech/vanlt/ss/slavery/linkspage.html Available July 13, 1999.

Johnson, Charles, Patricia Smith, and WGBH Research Team. *Africans in America: America's Journey through Slavery.* New York: Harcourt, Brace & Company, 1998, pp. 37–39, 42–46. This book is a companion to *Africans in America,* Public Broadcasting System, 1998. Videocassette recording.

Louis Jolliet

1645
Beauport, Canada
1700
Quebec, Canada

Explorer

Jacques Marquette

June 1, 1637
Laon, France
May 18, 1675
on Illinois River

Jesuit missionary

French-Canadian explorer Louis Jolliet and Jacques Marquette, a French Jesuit missionary, were the first Europeans to travel down the Mississippi River. Beginning their voyage in 1673, the two explorers traveled from New France (now Quebec) in French North America (now Canada), down the Mississippi to a point just north of the present border between Arkansas and Louisiana. Marquette became ill and could not continue the return trip. He died two years later, but his journal provided a valuable record of the expedition. Jolliet went on to explore the Hudson Bay in 1679, as well as the coast of Labrador (a peninsula between Newfoundland and Quebec) in 1689 and 1694. Engaged in trade with Native American groups he issued warnings about English traders that foreshadowed eighteenth-century conflicts between England and France.

Enters fur trade

Louis Jolliet was born in the town of Beauport, in the colony of New France in 1645. He was the son of a craftsman who died while Jolliet was still a child. His mother was widowed twice before she married Jolliet's father. The couple set-

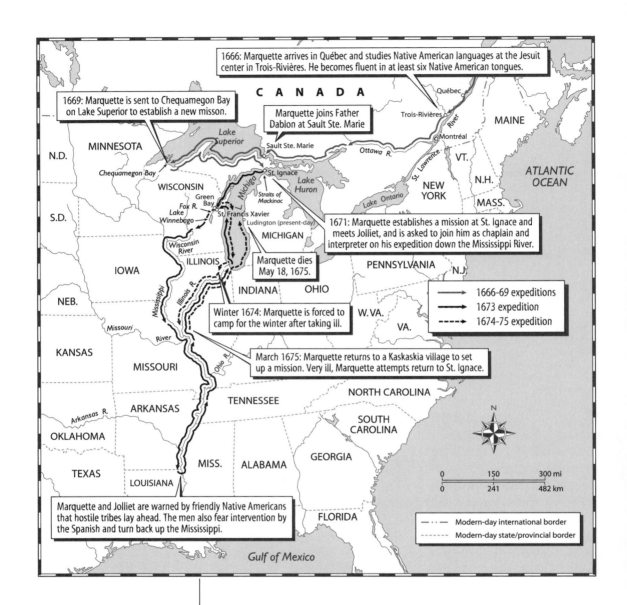

1666: Marquette arrives in Québec and studies Native American languages at the Jesuit center in Trois-Rivières. He becomes fluent in at least six Native American tongues.

1669: Marquette is sent to Chequamegon Bay on Lake Superior to establish a new misson.

Marquette joins Father Dablon at Sault Ste. Marie

CANADA

1671: Marquette establishes a mission at St. Ignace and meets Jolliet, and is asked to join him as chaplain and interpreter on his expedition down the Mississippi River.

Marquette dies May 18, 1675.

Winter 1674: Marquette is forced to camp for the winter after taking ill.

March 1675: Marquette returns to a Kaskaskia village to set up a mission. Very ill, Marquette attempts return to St. Ignace.

→ 1666-69 expeditions
→ 1673 expedition
---→ 1674-75 expedition

Marquette and Jolliet are warned by friendly Native Americans that hostile tribes lay ahead. The men also fear intervention by the Spanish and turn back up the Mississippi.

N

0   150   300 mi
0   241   482 km

—·—·— Modern-day international border
------- Modern-day state/provincial border

Map of the eastern United States showing the routes followed by Marquette and Jolliet.

tled in Beauport, near Quebec City. At the age of eleven Jolliet entered the Jesuit college in Quebec. There he studied philosophy and prepared to enter the priesthood. He also studied music and played the organ at the cathedral in Quebec for many years. In 1666 he defended a thesis before Bishop François Xavier de Laval of Quebec. The bishop was so impressed by Jolliet's work that he became one of the young man's principal financial supporters.

In 1667 Jolliet gave up his seminary studies and borrowed money from Laval to spend a year in France. During his stay he studied hydrography (the science of charting bodies of water). Upon his return to Quebec he entered the fur trade, which was the main business in New France. He was also one of the signers of a document in which the French claimed possession of the Great Lakes region. The French would enter into conflicts with the English over this prosperous area of trade during the eighteenth century. Pennsylvania fur trader **George Croghan** (see entry) would become instrumental in the success of the English in this region.

Meets Marquette

In 1672 Jolliet was chosen to lead an expedition to search for the Mississippi River. He was selected by the two highest officials in New France, Louis de Baude, Count de Frontenac, the governor, and Jean Talon, the intendant (administrator). The French learned of the existence of the river through reports from their Native American trading partners. They were uncertain, however, whether the river emptied into the Gulf of Mexico or farther west, into the Gulf of California.

Jolliet's party left Quebec on October 4, 1672. By early December they had reached the mission and trading post at Michilimackinac, which is now the town of St. Ignace on the Mackinac Peninsula between Lake Huron and Lake Michigan. Jolliet and his party remained at the mission for the winter. During his stay, he met the priest in charge of the mission, Father Jacques Marquette. Jolliet had brought instructions that Marquette was to accompany him on his voyage in order to preach to Native American tribes along the way. Marquette had settled in New France in 1666. There Jesuits were actively founding missions and converting Native Americans. Initially, Marquette's most important accomplishments were learning six Native American languages and founding a mission at St. Ignace (in present-day Michigan) in 1671.

Explore northern Mississippi

In May 1673 Jolliet and Marquette left Michilimackinac with five men and two canoes. They probably traveled

Marquette and Jolliet being greeted by the Illinois Indians during their exploration of the Mississippi River.
Reproduced by permission of The Granger Collection.

westward along the north shore of Lake Michigan to present-day Green Bay, Wisconsin, then up the Fox River. From there they portaged (carried boats overland) to the Wisconsin River, and then descended to the Mississippi on June 15, 1673. During this voyage, they traveled down the Mississippi past the Missouri and Ohio Rivers. Jolliet and Marquette stopped at the mouth of the Arkansas River, about 450 miles south of the mouth of the Ohio River. This point is just north of the present boundary between Arkansas and Louisiana. Here they encountered the Quapaw tribe, from whom they heard reports of the Spanish approaching from the west. The unfriendliness of the Quapaws, as well as the knowledge that the Mississippi must run into the Gulf of Mexico, convinced the explorers to turn back without having reached the mouth of the Mississippi. As a result, they had explored only the northern portion of the river. During the trip Marquette kept a journal that provided a first-person account of the expedition.

Marquette dies on mission trip

In mid-July the expedition began the return trip up the Mississippi to the Illinois River, making the portage at Chicago into the southern part of Lake Michigan. Jolliet and Marquette separated at the Saint Francis Xavier mission at Green Bay. Jolliet went on to Montreal to report on their discoveries, but Marquette had become ill, requiring him to stay at the mission. By the summer of 1674 he had recovered and had set out to fulfill a promise to build a mission for the Kaskasia tribe in present-day Illinois. By fall Marquette's illness had returned, however, and he was forced to spend the winter at a camp on a site in what is now suburban Chicago. On March 30, 1675, he continued his journey, traveling to a village on the Illinois River. On the Thursday before Easter he preached a sermon to a gathering of two thousand members of the Illinois nation. Although Marquette was quite ill by this time, he nevertheless tried to reach St. Ignace. He died along the way and was buried at the mouth of the river that was named for him, on the site of present-day Ludington, Michigan.

Jolliet encounters rapids

In the meantime, Jolliet had spent the winter of 1673–74 at Sault Sainte Marie (in present-day Upper Peninsula of Michigan), writing in his journal and making maps of the journey on the Mississippi River. Unfortunately, he later lost all of his papers when his canoe overturned on the Lachine Rapids near Montreal. The Lachine Rapids had first been spotted by French explorer **Jacques Cartier** (see entry) in 1535. After this disaster, Jolliet reached Quebec in the fall of 1674. He wrote another report of the trip entirely from memory. This narrative corresponds with Marquette's description, which is considered the official account of the journey.

Becomes active in fur trade

Once back in Quebec, Jolliet got married and became a fur merchant. He requested permission from the French government to establish a colony in the Illinois country, but France was reluctant to start any new ventures because its meager resources were already spread thin in New France. There-

Marquette describes Mississippi trip

In 1673 Louis Jolliet and Jacques Marquette discovered the Mississippi River. Marquette's journal provides a first-person account of their historic expedition. The following excerpt describes the sights they saw during the trip down the river.

> . . . we came into the Mississippi on the 17th of June.

> Behold us, then, upon this celebrated river, whose singularities I have attentively studied. The Mississippi takes its rise in several lakes in the North. . . . We slowly followed its course to the south and southeast to the 42° N. lat. Here we perceived the country change its appearance. There were scarcely any more woods or mountains. The islands are covered with fine trees, but we could not see any more roebucks [deer], buffaloes, bustards [game birds] and swans.

> We met from time to time monstrous fish, which struck so violently against our canoes, that at first we took them to be large trees, which threatened to upset us. We saw also a hideous monster; his head was like that of a tiger, his nose was sharp, and somewhat resembled a wildcat; his beard was long; his ears stood upright; the color of his head was gray; and his neck black. He looked upon us for some time, but as we came near him our oars frightened him away. . . .

> Having descended the river as far as 41° 28´ we found that turkeys took the place of game, and the Pisikious that of other animals. We called the Pisikious wild buffaloes, because they very much resemble our domestic oxen; they are not so long, but twice as large. We shot one of them, and it was as much as thirteen men could do to drag him from the place where he fell. . . .

fore, Jolliet devoted his efforts to the fur trade on the north shore of the St. Lawrence River.

In 1679 Jolliet led a mission to explore an overland route to the rich fur-trading regions of Hudson Bay, which were being exploited by the English at the time. When he reached Hudson Bay he encountered English traders and observed the extent of their business activities. Upon his return to Quebec, he wrote a report saying that the French risked losing the fur trade if they allowed the English to continue trading in the area. As a reward for his successful mission, Jolliet was given trading rights and land on the north shore. He also was awarded Anticosti Island, which is located in the middle of the Gulf of St. Lawrence. Although there are few details about Jolliet's later life, it is known that he had a successful career in the fur and fish trades on the St. Lawrence. He also embarked on several expeditions, including a mission

As we were descending the river we saw high rocks with hideous monsters painted on them, and upon which the bravest Indians dare not look. They are as large as a calf, with head and horns like a goat; their eyes red; beard like a tiger's; and a face like a man's. Their tails are so long that they pass over their heads and between their fore legs, under their belly, and ending like a fish's tail. They are painted red, green, and black. They are so well drawn that I cannot believe they were drawn by the Indians. And for what purpose they were made seems to me a great mystery.

As we fell down the river, and while we were discoursing upon these monsters, we heard a great rushing and bubbling of waters, and small islands of floating trees coming from the mouth of the Pekitanoni [Missouri River], with such rapidity that we could not drink it. It so discolors the Mississippi as to make the navigation of it dangerous. This river comes from the north-west, and empties into the Mississippi, and on its banks are situated a number of Indian villages. We judged by the compass, that the Mississippi discharged itself into the Gulf of Mexico.

Having satisfied ourselves, we resolved to return home. We considered that the advantage of our travels would be altogether lost to our nation if we fell into the hands of the Spaniards, from whom we could expect no other treatment than death or slavery.

Reprinted in: Colbert, David, ed. Eyewitness to America: 500 Years of America in the Words of Those Who Saw It. *New York: Pantheon Books, pp. 31–32.*

to the coast of Labrador in 1689. In addition, Jolliet was named royal professor of hydrography at the Jesuit college in Quebec in 1992.

Explores Labrador

In 1694 Jolliet was commissioned to return to Labrador to map the coastline. Leaving Quebec on April 28, he sailed along the north shore and the coast of Labrador until he reached the settlement of Zoar in July. Jolliet drew the first maps of the area, described the landscape, and gathered information about the Inuit (Eskimo) inhabitants. He noted that the main economic resources in Labrador were whale oil and seal oil, which could be traded with the Inuit. In October 1694 he returned to Quebec, only to discover that Anticosti Island had been seized by the English during his absence. He died during the summer of 1700.

For further research

Art in the U.S. Capitol: Jacques Marquette. http://www.aoc.gov/art/nshpages/marquett.htm Available July 13, 1999.

Colbert, David, ed. *Eyewitness to America: 500 Years of America in the Words of Those Who Saw It.* New York: Pantheon Books, pp. 31–32.

Father Jacques Marquette National Memorial and Museum. http://www.uptravel.com/uptravel/attractions/3.htm Available July 13, 1999.

Hamilton, Raphael N. *Father Marquette.* Detroit: William B. Eerdmans Publisher, 1970.

Kent, Zachary. *Jacques Marquette and Louis Jolliet.* Chicago: Children's Press, 1994.

Vachon, André. Louis Jolliet. In *Dictionary of Canadian Biography,* Volume 1. Toronto: University of Toronto, 1967.

William Kidd

c. 1645
Greenock, Scotland
May 23, 1701
Newgate, England

Privateer turned pirate

William Kidd (known as "Captain Kidd") was one of most famous pirates (a person who robs ships or plunders the land from the sea) in history. Before becoming a great plunderer (a person who steals by force) of the seas, he was a respectable colonial American citizen. In 1695 he was hired by English investors as a privateer (a sailor on a privately owned ship that is authorized by a government to attack and capture enemy vessels) to rid the seas of pirates. During the expedition, however, Kidd began attacking the very ships he was supposed to protect. After murdering one of his own crew members, Kidd was eventually tried and hanged in England in 1701. The value of the treasure of his biggest prize, the *Quedagh Merchant*, has become one of the famous myths about "Captain Kidd."

Hired to lead expedition

William Kidd, was born in Greenock, Scotland, around 1645 and was believed to be the son of a Calvinist (Calvinists placed strong emphasis on the supreme power of God, the sinfulness of mankind, and the doctrine of predestination, which states that all human events are controlled by God) minister.

"My Lord, it is a very hard sentence. For my part I am the innocentest person of them all. . . . "

William Kidd

Portrait: William (Captain) Kidd.
Reproduced by permission of Archive Photos, Inc.

169

Blackbeard the pirate

Blackbeard was another infamous English pirate. Although he was not a contemporary of William Kidd, his career began under similar circumstances. Blackbeard (whose real name was probably Edward Teach) was hired as a privateer during the War of Spanish Succession (1701–14; a conflict involving Britain, the Netherlands, and the Hapsburgs of Austria against France and Spain). After the war he became a pirate and was notoriously cruel. He had headquarters in the Bahamas and the Carolinas. Between 1716 and 1718 Blackbeard plundered ships and coastal settlements in the West Indies and along the east coast of North America. Blackbeard acquired some protection by sharing his treasure with the governor of North Carolina. However, in 1718 he was killed by a British force from Virginia. Like Kidd, Blackbeard became a legendary figure.

Portrait: Blackbeard (Edward Teach). *Reproduced by permission of Corbis-Bettmann.*

Before becoming a pirate, he was a resident of Boston, Massachusetts, an established shipowner in New York City, and the commander of a trading vessel in the West Indies. He also served in the war between England and France that took place after William of Orange (King William III) succeeded to the British throne. For his services, Kidd received a reward of 150 pounds (monetary units of the United Kingdom) from the House of Commons in 1691. Soon afterwards, he married Sarah Oort, who was the daughter of Captain Samuel Bradley and the widow of sea captain John Oort. The Kidds owned a great deal of property in New York, including a luxurious home and a country estate.

In 1695 the East India Company asked William III to send ships to the Indian Ocean and the Red Sea to defeat pirates that were attacking their company ships. Because the war with France was still in progress, there were no English ships available. As a result, the king decided to hire a privateer. During the same year, Richard Coote, Earl of Bellomont, was appointed governor of the Massachusetts Bay Colony. The king gave him the task of suppressing piracy (robbery on the high seas). Bellomont then consulted with Robert Livingston, a prominent New Yorker businessman. Livingston in turn met Kidd, who was in London at the time, and they began planning the expedition to the Indian Ocean. It was decided that Bellomont and a group of investors would pay for most of the trip and receive most of the profits. Kidd and Livingston were to pay the rest. Kidd then signed a contract to become commander of the expedition.

Becomes a pirate

On April 23, 1696, Kidd and several crew members left Plymouth, England, and sailed for New York on board the *Adventure Galley*. In New York, he picked up more crew members, so his ship now had 155 men on board. Leaving New York on September 16, 1696, Kidd sailed around the Cape of Good Hope by December, en route to Madagascar. He claimed he knew where to find pirates in Madagascar, which was their favorite hiding place. For some unspecified reason, however, he avoided the east coast where the pirates usually hid and instead sailed for the west coast. Kidd encountered problems when he reached the Comoro Islands in February. His crew was dying of cholera (a disease marked by severe gastrointestinal problems), the ship began to leak, and he had yet to capture any pirates.

At this point the crew threatened mutiny (rebellion). As a result, Kidd decided to become a pirate and to plunder the very ships he was sent to protect. Anxious to make money, his crew went along with his decision. He staged an unsuccessful attack in August, then managed to capture some ships a month later. But when he refused to attack a Dutch ship, a small mutiny took place. During the chaos Kidd killed William Moore, one of his gunners, by hitting him with a bucket. After this incident, there was no turning back for Kidd. Now a full-fledged pirate, he captured the *Quedagh Merchant* on January 30, 1698. Kidd then left the *Adventure* behind and, with a crew of fellow pirates, sailed on his newly acquired ship. Ironically,

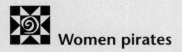

Women pirates

At least two women—Anne Bonney and Mary Read—are known to have been pirates. Bonney was the illegitimate daughter of an Irish attorney. She frequented the waterfront in Charleston, South Carolina, wearing men's clothing. In 1719 she eloped with James Bonney to the Bahamas, where she fell in love with a pirate named Calico Jack Rackham. He offered to buy a divorce from her husband. When James Bonney refused, Anne Bonney and Rackham seized a Dutch ship (the crew members supposedly were ignorant of her gender). Aboard the ship was Mary Read, who was disguised as a male sailor.

Mary Read was born in England and joined the Royal Navy when she was fourteen. She served her country with distinction during the War of the Spanish Succession (1701–14). After the war Read signed to serve on the Dutch ship. When the vessel was captured by Rackham and

Bonney, Read joined their crew. Bonney soon discovered Read's identity and the two became friends. When Read fell in love with a crew member she made her gender public. Then her lover quarreled with a shipmate and the two men went ashore to settle their differences. An experienced swordswoman, Read insisted on taking her lover's place and killed her opponent in a struggle.

In 1720 the ship was captured by the Royal Navy. The entire crew, including Bonney and Read, were sentenced to hang. Asked whether the condemned had anything to say, Bonney and Read reportedly shouted, "Milord, we plead our bellies!"—both women were pregnant. Since British law forbade the execution of pregnant women, their sentences were commuted (changed) to imprisonment. Bonney is said to have delivered her baby and escaped, never to be seen again. Read died of fever while being held in captivity.

he even befriended pirates named Culliford and Kelly, whom he was supposed to apprehend.

Tried as a pirate

By 1698 rumors had reached England that Kidd himself was a pirate. Leaving Madagascar in September 1698, Kidd arrived in the West Indies in April 1699. It was then that he discovered English authorities knew about his criminal activities. When Kidd received this news, he left the *Quedagh Merchant* in Hispaniola (an island in the Caribbean Sea) and sailed for New

England on board the *Antonio.* After anchoring in Oyster Bay (an inlet of Long Island Sound) he proclaimed his innocence to Bellomont. Bellomont arrested Kidd, however, and took the pirate to Boston. On July 2, Kidd appeared before the council and was thrown into jail. Later Kidd and his men were sent to London as prisoners.

After being examined by the British Board of Admiralty on April 14, 1700, Kidd was sent to the prison at Newgate. He waited there for over a year, until he was examined by the House of Commons on March 27, 1701. On May 8, he went to trial and was found guilty of the murder of Moore, as well as for the plundering of six ships. In his own defense, Kidd argued that two of the ships had French passes and were therefore captured legally. He also claimed that the passes were taken from him and concealed. Although Kidd pleaded his innocence, he was sentenced to death. On May 23, 1701, Kidd was hanged.

Myths about buried treasure

Like most pirates, Kidd's story is full of both fact and fiction. For instance, it is a fact that his fortune, which was transferred to the Crown (the royal government) after his execution, only amounted to 6,471 pounds. There is a great deal of fiction, however, about the size of the fortune on the *Quedagh Merchant.* After discovering that he was being sought as a pirate in 1698, Kidd left the large ship at Hispaniola and sailed to Boston on the *Antonio.* English authorities, however, were very anxious to know exactly where the *Quedagh Merchant* was located because it was believed to contain a fortune worth 70,000 pounds. Kidd brought some of the fortune back with him on the *Antonio,* but he gave no information about the remainder. As a result, many stories arose about where the treasure was buried and how much it was worth. Over the years, as treasure hunters tried and failed to find it, its worth became greatly exaggerated.

For further research
Ritchie, Robert C. *Captain Kidd and the War against the Pirates.* Cambridge, Mass.: Harvard University Press, 1986.

Whipple, Addison B. *The Mysterious Voyage of Captain Kidd.* New York: Random House, 1970.

Eusebio Francisco Kino

c.1644
Segno in Tyrol, Austria (now Italy)
March 15, 1711
Mission at Santa Magdalena

Jesuit missionary and explorer

Eusebio Francisco Kino was a pioneering seventeenth-century Jesuit missionary. He was also an explorer, mathematician, mapmaker, astronomer, and businessman. In 1665 Kino joined the Jesuits to train as a missionary. (Jesuits are members of the Society of Jesus, a Roman Catholic religious order for men founded by St. Ignatius of Loyola. They are dedicated to academic study and the establishment of foreign missions and schools.) Three years later he participated in an expedition to establish Spanish settlements in Mexico. Beginning in 1687, he spent almost twenty-five years in Primería Alta (the area that is now northern Mexico and southern Arizona), building missions and exploring the southwestern region of North America. His explorations led to the return of the Jesuits to the present-day Baja Peninsula of California in 1697. Kino was also responsible for establishing ranching as a viable economic enterprise in Primería Alta.

Establishes settlements

Eusebio Francisco Kino was born in 1644 in Segno in the Austrian province of Tyrol (now Italy). He was baptized on

August 10 the following year. As a young man, Kino received a good education. At a time when many people could not read or write, he studied at the universities of Inglostadt and Freiburg, where he showed an aptitude for mathematics. Although he was offered a professorship in mathematics at the University of Inglostadt, Kino had already decided his future was with the Roman Catholic Church. In 1665 he joined the Jesuits in order to become a missionary. Kino also continued studying mathematics in hopes of someday going to China.

Although it had been his dream for many years to go to China, Kino was sent to Mexico. After going to Cadíz, Spain, in 1678, he sailed on to Vera Cruz, Mexico, in 1681. At the time, Spain had decided to establish settlements in Baja California. The responsibility for this enterprise fell to the Jesuits, and Kino was selected to be one of two missionaries sent to California in 1683. Kino and his party spent two years exploring the region and making frequent reports. When a drought forced the cancellation of the enterprise in 1685, Kino was sent to Primería Alta.

A man of many talents

In addition to being a Jesuit missionary, Eusebio Kino was a man of many talents and abilities. For instance, his proficiency in mathematics won him the position of royal astronomer (a person who specializes in the study of space) and mapmaker. As an astronomer he published *Exposición Astronómica de el Cometa* (*Astronomical Exposition of the Comet*), a book about the comet of 1680, which he had observed while in Càdiz, Spain. He was also a noted explorer. After leading the Jesuits back to present-day Baja California in 1697, Kino discovered that the area was a peninsula rather than an island. His map of the region became quite popular and was published several times in Europe.

Establishes missions, explores Southwest

After arriving in Primería Alta in March 1687, Kino spent his time living and traveling among the Yuma and Pima Indians. As yet there were no European settlers in the area and he explored the region, built missions, and attended to his religious duties. Moving from his previous mission at the town of Cucurpe, he founded the mission of Nuestra Señora de los Dolores. Kino remained at Dolores from 1687 until 1711, from that location establishing missions in the Santa Cruz, San Miguel, Magdelena, San Pedro, Sonóita, and Altar river valleys. Some of these missions eventually grew into modern-day towns and cities. For instance, in April 1700 he

Spain needs California

When Eusebio Francisco Kino arrived in North America in 1681, Spain had already claimed present-day California but had not yet explored the land. By that time, mapping and settling the territory had become crucial. The Spanish conquest of the Philippines in the 1650s had opened trade between Mexico and Manila across the Pacific Ocean. But the present route from Mexico to the Philippines skirted California because ships had to avoid dangerous currents. Moreover, English and Dutch pirates (people who rob ships and the land from the sea) lay in wait, hoping to plunder rich Spanish ships. Spain therefore needed a harbor on the coast so the voyage would be safer and more direct. The Spanish government also wanted to take advantage of the abundant pearl fishing in California waters. Yet, earlier in the century the Spaniards had alienated Native American tribes in the Southwest, so no permanent Spanish settlements had been built. Kino's party was sent to explore the area, befriend the Native Americans, and establish missions.

founded San Xavier del Bac, which is now Tucson, Arizona.

Kino did more than direct the building of missions. He also led explorations that pushed as far north as the Gila and Colorado Rivers and which ultimately led to the return of the Jesuits to the Baja Peninsula of California in 1697. Up until this time the area was believed to be an island, but Kino confirmed that it was actually a peninsula and could therefore be reached and explored by land. Kino traveled thousands of miles on horseback, sometimes with Europeans and other times with Native Americans. In 1695 he rode to Mexico City, taking 53 days to make the 1,500-mile journey.

Establishes ranching as a business

Kino was also a skilled businessman. He is credited with introducing ranching as a viable economic enterprise in Primería Alta. The older missions had supplied him with a few animals, but he went on to establish cattle ranches in at least six river valleys in northern Mexico. The missions bred cattle, horses, mules, and sheep. The animals not only fed Native Americans but also enabled the missions to be financially self-sufficient. This was an important factor because it meant that the missions could survive regardless of what was happening politically and economically in Spain. In addition, it allowed Kino to develop new missions without relying on help from anybody else. For example, when creating San Xavier del Bac he was able to send along seven hundred animals—a large herd for the time. He also originated the idea of building a road around the head of the Gulf of Mexico in order to shorten the

A Jesuit missionary, like Eusebio Francisco Kino, preaching to Native Americans in Texas. *Reproduced by permission of The Granger Collection.*

water route for shipping livestock. One historian has credited Kino with establishing the cattle industry in at least twenty places where it still exists today, including Tucson.

Remains devout to the end

Kino seems to have exemplified the simplicity and faith that marked the most devout Jesuits. He took his vows of poverty seriously, owning few possessions, and he ate and slept sparingly. He was unafraid to die, secure in his belief in the promise of salvation (forgiveness of sins). He died on March 15, 1711, during a visit to dedicate a chapel at the mission of Santa Magdalena. Luis Velarde, Kino's companion for the last eight years of his life, wrote: "He died as he had lived, with extreme humility and poverty. In token of this, during his last illness he did not undress. His deathbed, as his bed had always been, consisted of two calfskins for a mattress, two blankets such as the Indians use for covers, and a pack-saddle for a pillow."

For further research

Bolton, Herbert Eugene. *Kino's Historical Memoir of Primería Alta,* Volume 1. Cleveland: Arthur H. Clark, 1919.

"Eusebio Kino, S.J." http://www.library.arizona.edu/images/swf/kino.html Available July 13, 1999.

Johnson, Allen, and others, ed. *Dictionary of American Biography.* New York: Scribner, 1946–1958, pp. 419–20.

Sarah Kemble Knight

April 19, 1666
Boston, Massachusetts
September 25, 1727
New London, Connecticut

Colonial diarist and businesswoman

Sarah Kemble Knight is best known as the author of *The Journal of Madame Knight* (published in 1825), an account of her journey through New England in 1704. Her remarkable diary provides a detailed portrait of the landscape and culture of early colonial Connecticut and New York. It also reveals Knight's own strong personality, which enabled her to transcend the limitations placed on women. For instance, at that time many women could not read or write, let alone take on a difficult journey through the wilderness. In addition to writing the journal, Knight was a successful businesswoman and legal advisor.

Active in business and law

Sarah Kemble Knight was born on April 19, 1666, in Boston, Massachusetts, to Thomas Kemble and Elizabeth (Trerice) Kemble. Her mother was the daughter of Nicholas Trerice, a shipowner in Charlestown, Massachusetts. Her father was a merchant who owned land in the area that is now Maine. As a young woman, Knight acquired the good education that enabled her to write her famous diary and to participate in business and legal activities. Before her father died in

> "I thought it proper to warn poor Travailers to endeavor to Avoid falling into circumstances like ours. . . . "
>
> *Sarah Kemble Knight*

179

1689, she married much older Richard Knight, a widower and shipowner. The couple had one child, Elizabeth.

Upon the death of her father, Knight took over as head of his household and ran a boarding house, where many of her relatives lived. In addition, she engaged in legal activities such as assisting in settling estates and recording public documents. Historians have found hundreds of official papers that bear her signature as well as court records presumably written in her hand. There is little evidence, however, to support the popular claim that she taught the future scientist and statesman **Benjamin Franklin** (see entry) at the writing school she operated from 1706 to 1713. Historians speculate that Knight's husband died in 1706.

Embarks on difficult journey

Because of her legal skills, Knight took on many business responsibilities. In 1704 one of the boarders at her Boston residence married her cousin, Caleb Trowbridge, who lived in New Haven, Connecticut. Trowbridge died within two months after the marriage. In October of the same year, Knight set out for New Haven to assist Trowbridge's widow in legal matters. The trip through the wilderness from Boston to New Haven was extremely difficult and hazardous. For a woman to undertake such a journey alone—and on horseback—was considered unthinkable at the time. (Knight followed the route now used by the Pennsylvania Central Railroad.)

Since there were very few roads or bridges along the way, Knight had to seek the help of guides. Despite encountering hardships, she gave a lighthearted and sometimes humorous account of the trip in her diary. She recorded all the "Bugbears to a fearful female travailer," such as "Bridges which were . . . very tottering and of vast Length." When bridges were lacking, Knight crossed rivers in canoes or on horseback. After traveling for five days, she arrived at New Haven. Along the way she had recorded a vivid portrait of colonial America, which enlightens and entertains readers even today.

Knight described the farmhouses and inns where she stayed. She also wrote about the country people and their local dialects, and she commented about the food and lodging she received. She provided a vivid account of the culture in New

WILLIAM PARKHURST HORSHAM
SUSSEX COMMON STAGE WAG
TO THE TALBOT INN BOROUGH

TALBOT INN

Haven, where she remained for two months. During this time, she met Thomas Trowbridge, who was probably the father of Caleb, and decided to accompany him to New York City. They arrived there in three days, and Knight once again wrote about the local culture. After finishing their business in New York, Knight and Trowbridge returned to New Haven. Knight then proceeded on to Boston in late February, arriving there in early March. Her account of this journey was more general than the previous one.

Sarah Kemble Knight made her journey from Boston to New Haven in a covered wagon much like the ones pictured here in front of a colonial inn.
Illustration by Philip Norman.

Becomes famous years later

Although Knight did not receive fame for her journal during her lifetime, she became known for her other accomplishments. Her mother died in 1712, and her daughter Elizabeth was married the following year to Colonel John Livingston from New London, Connecticut. When the newlyweds moved to Connecticut, Knight sold her property in

Knight visits the "Devil's Habitation"

Wednesday, October 4th. [1704]

About four in the morning, we set out for Kingston [Massachusetts] (for so was the Town called) with a french Docter in our company. Hee and the Post put on very furiously, so that I could not keep up with them, only as now and then they'd stop till they see mee. This Rode was poorly furnished with accommodations for Travellers, so that we were forced to ride 22 miles by the post's account, but neerer thirty by mine, before wee could bait so much as our Horses, which I exceedingly complained of. But the post encourag'd mee, by saying wee should be well accommodated anon [soon] at Mr. Devills, a few miles further. But I questioned whether we ought to go to the Devil to be helpt out of affliction. However, like the rest of Deluded souls that post to the Infernal denn, Wee made all possible speed to this Devil's Habitation; where alliting [alighting, or getting out of the coach], in full assurance of good accommodation, wee were going in. But meeting his two daughters, as I suposed twins, they so neerly resembled each other, both in features and habit, and look't as old as the Divel himselfe, and quite as Ugly, We desired entertainm't, but could hardly get a word out of 'um, till with our Importunity [request or demand], telling them our necesity, &c. they call'd the old Sophister, who was as sparing of his words as his daughters had bin, and no, or none, was the reply's hee made us to our demands. Hee differed only in this from the old fellow in to'ther Country: hee let us depart. However, I thought it proper to warn poor Travailers to endeavor to Avoid falling into circumstances like ours. . . .

Reprinted in: Gunn, Giles, ed. Early American Writing. *New York: Penguin, 1994, p. 270.*

Boston and went with them. She bought property in Norwich and New London. From 1714 until her death, she operated a shop and a house of entertainment, managed many farms, and conducted business with Native Americans. In 1718 she and several business owners were accused of selling liquor to local Native Americans. Although Knight blamed a servant for the deed, she was still forced to pay a fine. The incident did not affect her standing in society, however, and she continued to prosper, eventually amassing an estate worth 1800 pounds—a sizable fortune in those days. When Knight died on September 25, 1727, in New London, her property was apparently inherited by Elizabeth.

After Knight's death her journal passed into private hands and remained in manuscript form. About a hundred years later the diary was discovered by Theodor Dwight Jr., who had it published as *The Journal of Madame Knight* (1825). Over the years the book was reprinted a number of times and read by generations of new readers. *The Journal of Madame Knight* provides a more realistic portrait than most literature of the period. Presenting the vivid contrasts between wilderness and civilization, the diary describes a variety of cultures as well as the author's own buoyant personality in the face of hardship.

For further research

Elliott, Emory, and others, eds. *American Literature: A Prentice Hall Anthology*. Englewood Cliffs, New Jersey, 1991, pp. 235–36.

Gunn, Giles, ed. *Early American Writing*. New York: Penguin, 1994, p. 270.

James, Edward T., and others, eds. *Notable American Women, 1607–1950*, Volume II. Cambridge, MA: Belknap Press of Harvard University Press, 1971, pp. 340–41.

Johnson, Allen, and others, eds. *Dictionary of American Biography*. New York: Scribner, pp. 340–41.

Motion: A Travel Journal-Time Travelers: Sarah Kemble Knight (1666-1727). http://www.nearbycafe.com/motion/motionmenu/timetravel/knight.html Available July 13, 1999.

"Sarah Kemble Knight" in *The Puritans: American Literature Colonial Period (1608-1700)*. http://falcon.jmu.edu/-ramseyil/amicol.htm Available July 13, 1999.

Sigerman, Harriet, ed. *Young Oxford History of Women in the United States: Biographical Supplement and Index*. New York: Oxford University Press, 1994, pp. 92–93.

René-Robert Cavelier de La Salle

November 22, 1643
Rouen, France
March 19, 1687
Navosta, Texas

French explorer

Portrait: Rene-Robert Cavelier Sieur de La Salle. *Reproduced by permission of The Library of Congress.*

René-Robert Cavelier de La Salle was a celebrated French explorer who made great strides in the exploration of North America. As a young man he hoped to be a Jesuit missionary, but he became an explorer instead and later was vital as a builder of New France (present-day Quebec, Canada). After the French government granted La Salle the right to explore, trade, and construct forts in New France, he and his men set out across the Great Lakes in a specially built ship called the *Griffon.* During their journey they established many present-day cities in the Midwest and La Salle became the first European to sail down the Mississippi River to its mouth. Yet in spite of La Salle's success, he was responsible for several misadventures and disasters that directly led to his being killed in cold blood by his own men.

Raises money for expedition

René-Robert Cavelier de La Salle was born into a well-to-do family in Rouen, the capital of the French province of Normandy. He studied at a school run by Jesuits (a Roman Catholic religious order) in his hometown and then became a novice (a student who studies for the Catholic priesthood) at a Jesuit seminary in Paris, France. He showed an aptitude for mathematics and taught that subject to secondary school students while pursuing his own studies. La Salle was not a successful seminarian, however—the Jesuits thought he was too adventurous and unstable. After being turned down twice for a chance to be a missionary, he quit his religious studies in 1667.

La Salle had family connections in New France, so he moved there soon after leaving the seminary. Upon his arrival in Quebec, sometime before November 1667, he was granted a gift of land on the island of Montreal (located on the St. Lawrence River in Canada). Two years later he sold the land for a profit. With this money La Salle decided to lead an expedition to find the Ohio River, which he thought would lead to the South Seas and eventually to China.

Searches for Ohio River

La Salle's expedition attracted the attention of the Sulpicians, a Roman Catholic order that sent two of their members along to serve as missionaries. The party left Montreal in July 1669. Since none of the group had any exploring experience, the trip turned into a disaster. After crossing Lake Ontario, they were forced to spend a month in the village of the hostile Seneca tribe. They were finally rescued by an Iroquois who offered to guide them to the Ohio by way of Lake Erie. But before they got as far as Lake Erie, La Salle became sick with fever and the two missionaries were lured away to visit the Potawotami tribe.

Because of his illness, La Salle told his companions he was returning to Montreal. However, he did not reach the settlement until the fall of 1670. There is no record of his travels during 1669–70, but many of his later supporters claimed that he discovered the Ohio and Mississippi Rivers during this time. Evidence shows, however, that this is almost certainly not true and that the Mississippi was not found until 1673 by the French explorers **Louis Jolliet** and **Jacques Marquette** (see dual entry).

Explores American Southwest

La Salle made other unknown trips from 1671 to 1673. In the fall of 1673 he returned to Montreal. Once there, he allied himself with Louis de Buade (also known as the Count of Frontenac), the governor of New France, in a dispute that was then going on in the colony. For his support, La Salle was rewarded with a title of nobility (Sieur de La Salle) and command of Fort Frontenac at the site of present-day Kingston, Ontario. In 1677 he went back to France, and the following year he received permission from King Louis XIV to explore the western part of North America between New France, Florida, and Mexico.

The following September, La Salle started the expedition by constructing a fort on the Niagara River. He was accompanied by several other French explorers who were to gain fame as well, including Henry de Tonti and Louis Hennepin. La Salle was forced to spend the winter of 1678–79 at Fort Frontenac at Kingston. Upon his return he discovered that his men had built a ship, the *Griffon,* for exploration of the Great Lakes. They sailed on August 7, 1679.

Explores Great Lakes

The explorers traveled through Lake Erie into Lake Huron and then to Michilimackinac, a strip of land that separates Lake Huron from Lake Michigan. Leaving the *Griffon,* they went south on Lake Michigan in canoes. In the middle of winter they reached a village of the Illinois tribe near the present-day city of Peoria, Illinois. Discouraged by Native Americans from continuing, several of La Salle's men deserted. But La Salle built a fort called Crèvecoeur in the area to serve as a supply center for future explorations. He then sent Hennepin to lead an advance party to find the Mississippi River while La Salle headed back to Canada.

La Salle's return trip to Canada was beset by disaster after disaster: the *Griffon* got lost, then La Salle discovered the fort on the Niagara had been burned down and that a supply ship had sunk. At Fort Frontenac he learned that Crèvecoeur also had been destroyed by fire. Making matters even worse, many of his men had deserted and were returning to Canada, robbing his supply posts along the way. Setting an ambush, La Salle captured them at the beginning of August. He then retraced his route and went all the way back to Crèvecoeur, hoping to find Tonti, whom he had left in charge. Since Tonti was not among the corpses left behind at the burned fort, La

Salle assumed he was alive. When the two explorers finally met the following May, La Salle discovered that Tonti had escaped by rowing a canoe back to Michilimackinac.

Travels length of Mississippi

In 1681 La Salle returned once again to Montreal, where he tried to calm his creditors as well as defend himself against his enemies, who were spreading rumors about his mismanagement of the expedition. He then headed back into the wilderness with a party of forty men, reaching Fort Crèvecoeur in January 1682. From Crèvecoeur they descended the Illinois River, reaching the Mississippi River in February. They built canoes and rowed down the river, passing the mouth of the Missouri. La Salle finally sighted the Ohio River, which had been his goal when he set out on his first expedition thirteen years earlier. On the site of present-day Memphis, Tennessee, he also built a fort called Prud'homme.

In March, La Salle and his men were threatened with attack by a party from the Arkansas tribe. Averting a conflict, La Salle took possession of the country in the name of King Louis XIV. Leaving Prud'homme, La Salle's party continued down the river and passed the farthest point reached by Jolliet and Marquette. They spent time among the Tensas and Natchez tribes before reaching the Gulf of Mexico on April 9, 1682. He claimed the territory for France, calling it Louisiana and erecting a great cross.

As they started back upriver the next day, however, they were attacked by Native Americans and La Salle again became seriously ill. Remaining at Fort Prud'homme to recuperate, he sent Tonti on ahead to report back to the governor of New France on their discoveries. After a five-month recovery, La Salle continued his journey to Michilimackinac, where he was reunited Tonti and sent dispatches about his successful ventures in Quebec to France.

Recalled to France

In the meantime, while La Salle was recovering from his illness, a new governor had arrived in New France. The governor was quickly influenced by La Salle's enemies, who charged the explorer with mismanagement of the expedition and mistreatment of his men. On the governor's orders, La Salle was sent back to France in December 1683 to report on his conduct. He found little support in France for his ideas on developing the Mississippi valley. He did learn, however, that an important group was trying to interest the French government in sending an expedition to the mouth of the Rio Grande River in the Gulf of Mexico. Their plan was to seize valuable mines in New Mexico and New Spain (also part of present-day Mexico). In order to be a part of these schemes, La Salle purposely falsified his discoveries, virtually moving the Mississippi River from Louisiana to Texas. That is, he made a map that placed the Mississippi River much farther to the west and emptying into the Gulf of Mexico from Texas rather than Louisiana.

Heads expedition to Gulf of Mexico

With the help of his false maps, La Salle was able to convince the king and rich French merchants to sponsor an expedition to the Gulf of Mexico. He left France at the end of July 1684, heading a party of four ships and 327 men and women. As a result of bad planning and La Salle's ongoing quarrel with the naval captain, the ships were overloaded and there was not enough fresh water for the voyage. The party was forced to stop at the French colony of Haiti (an island in the Caribbean Sea). There they learned that one of their ships, which had been following with most of their supplies, had been captured by the Spanish.

Leaving Haiti with the three remaining ships in November, La Salle headed toward the Mississippi delta (a deposit of sand, gravel, clay and similar material at the mouth of a river). On December 27 and 28, they saw muddy waters that indicated they were near the mouth of the great river. La Salle had made miscalculations in his navigation, however, and followed old, unreliable Spanish charts. Therefore, instead of investigating the immediate area, he decided he was much farther east than he actually was and headed west.

Sails off course to Texas

By the time La Salle realized his mistake, the ships were off Matagorda Bay south of the site of present-day Houston, Texas. After one of the ships ran aground while sailing into the bay, local Native Americans tried to ransack the wreckage. The

Frenchmen shot at them, and from then on the two groups were enemies. In March the naval captain returned to France with one of his ships, leaving La Salle with only one vessel. By that time the remaining men were very discouraged, so La Salle was facing a tense situation.

In May 1685 La Salle constructed a fort at the mouth of the Lavaca River on Matagorda Bay. It was the only French colony to be established in the Southwest. With the fort as a

Tonti witnesses La Salle's death

In 1678 Henri de Tonti, an Italian explorer, joined René-Robert Cavelier de La Salle on a return trip to North America. Tonti's journal provides a valuable record of this historic expedition, which extended French power more than two thousand miles into the interior of the continent. In addition to chronicling the voyage to the mouth of the Mississippi River, Tonti gave an account of the Europeans' uneasy relations with Native Americans and the eventual mutiny of La Salle's men. Tonti described how they murdered La Salle:

Du Haut [a member of La Salle's party] and Lanquetot [the surgeon on the expedition] had for a long time determined to kill M. [Monsieur] de La Salle, because, during the journey he had made along the seacoast, he had compelled the brother of Lanquetot, who was unable to keep up, to return to camp, and as he was returning alone he was massacred by the savages [Native Americans]. This caused Lanquetot to swear that he would never forgive his brother's death. And, as in long journeys there are always many discontented persons in a company, he easily found partisans [supporters]. He offered therefore, with them, to search for M. de Morganet [La Salle's nephew], in order to have an opportunity to execute their design. . . .

According to Tonti, du Haut and Lanquetot found de Morganet with one of La Salle's servants and a Chaouanon

base, La Salle and several members of the party made exploring trips into the surrounding countryside. In April 1686, when a drunken captain wrecked the last ship, the little colony was left with no means of escape. La Salle decided the only way out was to travel overland to the Mississippi and then head up the river to the Great Lakes, where they could find French missions and traders. The party of twenty men left at the end of April. As a result of various mishaps, the number was reduced to eight by October, and La Salle was forced to return to the fort on the Lavaca.

Killed by his own men

La Salle set out again in January 1687 with seventeen companions, leaving twenty-five behind at the fort. By this time the men hated La Salle for causing them such misery. On the night of March 18 and 19, 1687, a group of five killed his

(Native American), all of whom they killed. Tonti continued the narrative:

> Towards daybreak [du Haut and Lanquetot] heard the reports [shots] of pistols, which were fired as signals by M. de La Salle, who was coming with the Recollect Father [Louis Hennepin, a Franciscan priest] in search of them. The wretches, suspecting that it was he, lay in wait for him, placing du Haut's servant in front. When M. de La Salle came near, he asked where M. de Morganet was. The servant [insolently] keeping on his hat, answered that he was behind. As M. de La Salle advanced to remind him of his duty, he received three balls in his head, and fell down dead (March 19, 1687).

> . . . Such was the end of one of the greatest men of an age, a man of admirable spirit, and capable of undertaking all sorts of explorations. . . .

Other witnesses to the murder were Hennipin and La Salle's brother (also a priest), who pleaded for their lives. Du Haut and Lanquetot finally agreed to spare the priests, but would not permit La Salle's brother to bury La Salle's body. Snatching the party's baggage, du Haut and Lanquetot fled to the village of a Natchez tribe. A few days later they themselves were killed in revenge for murdering La Salle and a Natchez chief.

Reprinted in: Stiles, T. J., ed. In Their Own Words: The Colonizers. New York: The Berkeley Publishing Group, 1998, p. 293.

nephew, servant, and guide. The next morning, at a spot just north of the modern town of Navosta, Texas, the rebellious group shot La Salle in cold blood. They left his body to be eaten by wild animals. The remaining members of La Salle's expedition reached Montreal on July 13, 1688.

For further research

Coulter, Tony. *La Salle and the Explorers of the Mississippi.* New York: Chelsea House, 1991.

Dupré, Céline. "Réne-Robert Cavelier de La Salle." *Dictionary of Canadian Biography,* Volume 1. Toronto: University of Toronto Press, 1967.

Osler, E. B. *La Salle.* Toronto: Longmans Canada, 1967.

Stiles, T. J., ed. *In Their Own Words: The Colonizers.* New York: The Berkeley Publishing Group, 1998, p. 293.

Terrell, John Upton. *The Life and Times of an Explorer.* London, England: Weybright and Talley, 1968.

Jacob Leisler

1640
Frankfurt, Germany
May 16, 1691
New York

Merchant, militia officer, and rebel

Jacob Leisler was a German merchant and militia officer who led a rebellion in New York (then New Netherland) in 1689. Driven by religious conviction, he tried to lessen Roman Catholic power in the colony. At the time the colony was made up of many diverse groups—rich and poor, Protestant and Catholic. The main conflict was between Protestants and other colonists—primarily the Dutch—who were joining the Church of England (the official religion of England; also known as the Anglican Church). Because of the long tradition of Calvinism in his family, Leisler wanted the Protestants to triumph because he believed the Anglican Church would eventually submit to Catholicism. (Calvinism was a branch of the Protestant religion that placed strong emphasis on the supreme power of God, the sinfulness of mankind, and the doctrine of predestination, which states that all human events are controlled by God.) While historians continue to debate Leisler's motivations for leading the rebellion, most of the evidence points to his intense religious beliefs.

Robert R. Livingston

Robert R. Livingston was the first prominent member of a family of important American political figures. He was born in Roxburgshire, Scotland, in 1654. After growing up in Holland, he emigrated (moved from one country to another) to the colony of New York (then New Netherland) in 1673. He settled in Albany and married Alida Van Rensselaer six years later. Livingston accumulated substantial wealth by trading goods with Native Americans. Under Governor Thomas Dongan, Livingston acquired a patent (title or deed) for 160,000 acres of land, which he turned into Livingston Manor.

Livingston was a major opponent of the 1689 rebellion led by militia officer Jacob Leisler. After the revolt was subdued, Livingston encountered problems with Leisler's followers who called themselves Leislerians. He had to defend himself against their rising power, which threatened his estates and privileges. A

Portrait: Robert A. Livingston. *Reproduced by permission of Francis Mayer/Corbis-Bettmann.*

highly respected citizen in the colony, Livingston served as secretary of Indian affairs until his death in 1728. Among his descendants is United States Congressman Robert Livingston, from Louisiana.

Influenced by Calvinist tradition

Jacob Leisler was born in 1640 in Frankfurt, Germany. His family, on both his father's and mother's sides, came from a long line of German *magistri* (magistrate or lawyer class). According to the founder of Calvinism, French Protestant reformer John Calvin, the *magistri* existed "to withstand the fierce licentiousness [disregard for rules of moral conduct] of kings in accordance with their duty." Many *magistri* became staunch Calvinist Christians, combining their legal duties with their religious beliefs. Leisler's grandfather relied upon

Calvinist teachings when he provided legal counsel to Prince Christian of Anhalt (a former state in Germany). He made sure that his own son, Leisler's father, received a solid religious education. Leisler's father later served as a Calvinist pastor to Huguenot (French Calvinist) exiles.

Leisler thus acquired a zealous Calvinistic view of the world, which included a deep fear of Roman Catholicism. Part of this concern resulted from the Catholic-Protestant conflicts during the Thirty Years War (1618–48; a general European war fought mainly in Germany), which had reached its most destructive stage at the time Leisler was born. Three years previously his parents had fled the Roman Catholic Inquisition (an official inquiry formed to discover and punish heretics, or those who disobeyed the laws of the Roman Catholic Church). Telling their son stories about this difficult time, the Leislers instilled in him a suspicion of Roman Catholicism. Jacob Leisler took this mistrust with him when he emigrated to New York in 1660.

Becomes prominent in New York

Leisler went to New York as a soldier in the Dutch West India Company (the trading and colonizing company that founded the colony of New Netherland, later called New York). After becoming a merchant he married a rich widow, and by 1676 he was one of the wealthiest men in the colony. Although Leisler had secured a high social position, he was unpopular with prominent Dutch families in New York. In 1674 he had spoken out against Nicholas Van Rensselaer, who was attempting to become a minister in the Dutch Reformed Church (now the Reformed Church of America; founded in Holland after the rise of Calvinism in the sixteenth century). Leisler was opposed to Van Rensselaer because he had been ordained by the Church of England. Leisler objected to Van Rensselaer's ties with the Church of England because Calvinists feared that England would be taken over by Catholics. As a deacon (layman, or unordained person, elected to assist the pastor of a church) of a Calvinist congregation, Leisler therefore opposed any Catholic influence in the church at a time when Protestantism was unstable in the colony.

Despite his strong Calvinist beliefs, Leisler served under New York's Catholic governor Thomas Dongan. In 1683

Dongan appointed Leisler as a Court of Admiralty commissioner, hoping Leisler could help ease tensions among diverse Protestant groups. Although he resented working for a Catholic, Leisler agreed to serve in this capacity. His concern about the instability of Protestantism and the rising dominance of Catholicism was intensified in 1685 when French king Louis XIV revoked the Edict of Nantes (a decree issued in 1598, which defined the rights of Protestants). Another blow to Protestant hopes came during the same year when King James II, a Catholic, ascended the throne of England.

From this time onward Leisler became more radical in his Protestantism. Like his ancestors, he combined his secular (public) duties and religious beliefs, viewing political action as spiritual warfare. He believed that Anglicans were too willing to submit to Catholicism, especially after New York came under the Dominion of New England (a self-governing nation in the British Commonwealth) during the reign of James II. During this time, many other Protestant groups, who would not normally have been in a close alliance with Leisler, began to see him as their spokesman. As a result, a strong anti-Catholic coalition was developing in New York, with Leisler at the head.

Takes over Fort James

In 1688 the Protestants of New York received news that James II had a son. Now the prospects of a long Catholic rule in England were a reality. But the situation was changed when William III, the Protestant husband of James II's

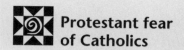

Protestant fear of Catholics

The situation in New York during Jacob Leisler's tenure as Court of Admiralty commissioner is an example of the profound impact of the Protestant Reformation—and the subsequent fear of Catholicism—on the American colonies. The Reformation was a revolution within, and ultimately against, the Roman Catholic Church that swept Western Europe in the sixteenth century. The movement began as early as the fourteenth century, however. Martin Luther, a Catholic professor of theology at the University of Wittenberg in Germany, is credited with starting the Reformation. On October 31, 1517, Luther posted 95 theses, or charges, on the door of the castle church in Wittenberg. In the theses he demanded reform within the Catholic Church. Specifically, he accused the Catholic clergy (priests, bishops, and popes) of gross corruption and misuse of power. Luther's action led to the founding of Lutheranism, the first Protestant denomination, or group of congregations. Luther was followed in the 1530s by the French reformer John Calvin, who founded Calvinism. From that time onward the Protestant movement gained momentum, fueling fears and animosities against Catholics throughout the world.

Bacon's Rebellion of 1676

Rebellions like Leisler's were common in colonial America, as less powerful individuals rose up against aristocrats (members of the ruling class or nobility). Another significant uprising was Bacon's Rebellion in 1676. Led by landowner **Nathaniel Bacon** (see entry), colonists staged a revolt in Jamestown, Virginia. At the time the colony was ruled by British governor **William Berkeley** (see entry), who focused primarily on his own economic interests at the expense of colonists. When Berkeley refused to continue defending Jamestown against Native Americans in order to protect the fur trade, Bacon led the Virginians in an uprising. At the end of the conflict, on September 18, 1676, Bacon burned Jamestown to the ground. Historians believe that Bacon's main target was Berkeley, while Leisler's rebellion involved religion and the common man against an aristocratic elite.

daughter Mary II, invaded England. Protestant hopes were now revived in both England and America. Francis Nicholson, lieutenant governor of the Dominion of New England, tried to keep William III's invasion a secret from American colonists. Eventually, however, Leisler received the news and made it public. New Englanders, who had long objected to the Dominion governor, Edmund Andros, because he was an overbearing and dictatorial governor, now saw their chance to overthrow him. Now that Andros had no backing in England and could not defend himself against a rebellion, the colonists sent him and other officials to England as prisoners. When the rebellion reached New York, Nicholson appointed Leisler to end the uprising. Leisler accepted this official position, hoping to apply his Calvinist beliefs to the colonial government.

Soon after his appointment, however, Leisler learned that the lieutenant governor had supported James II. Therefore, Leisler reversed his support for Nicholson. He had also heard about a possible anti-Protestant plot between Andros and Nicholson. Leisler was reluctant to rise up against Nicholson until he realized that it was his duty as a Calvinist to fight. In 1689, when Nicholson went to England seeking support, Leisler seized New York City's Fort James with a group of militiamen (a citizen army).

After this move, many colonists hailed Leisler as a defender of the Protestant faith. He was soon named lieutenant governor of the colony and upon gaining power he declared his allegiance to Protestant king William III. Leisler believed his authority had been confirmed by a letter sent by the king in December 1688. Addressed to Nicholson or whoever may have been in command at the time, Leisler automatically assumed the letter granted him the power to take over command of the colony. Thus he continued to occupy Fort James, feeling confident that William III approved of his rebellion.

Attempts to gain wider support

In spite of his victory, Leisler was not widely supported by other colonists. For instance, when he held a meeting for various representatives of the colony in 1689, no one attended. Leisler was also hindered by his unpopularity among prominent Dutch families, who resented the fact that the colony was now governed by a group of lowly traders. As a result, Leisler was backed mainly by poor merchants and farmers. He attempted to gain wider support twice in 1690. In February he launched a military expedition to protect northern New York. The militia arrived too late, however, and sixty colonists were killed by French soldiers and Native Americans. In his second attempt to gain support, Leisler called a meeting in April to negotiate with colonists who had protested against his high taxes. Nevertheless, while attempting to please one group of colonists, he ended up angering another. In the end, Leisler still had not won over prominent families who doubted his ability to govern.

Stands trial as a traitor

Not surprisingly, Leisler's victory for the Protestants was short-lived. The tables finally turned when certain merchants, who had been harmed by his economic policies, convinced William III that Leisler was a traitor. In December 1689 the king appointed Colonel Henry Sloughter to replace Leisler as governor of New York. Sloughter did not arrive from England until 1691 because his ship had been delayed by a storm. Accompanied by hundreds of troops, he tried to take command peacefully but Leisler refused to hand over Fort James. The confrontation resulted in violence, and during the fighting several English soldiers were killed. Leisler finally surrendered the fort. Outraged by Leisler's rebelliousness, Sloughter ordered him to stand trial for treason. Leisler defended himself by claiming that William III's letter of December 1689 had given him the authority to take over Fort James. His accusers argued, however, that command should immediately have been turned over to the council after Nicholson's departure.

On March 31, 1691, Leisler was found guilty of treason. According to records, on May 16, 1691, Leisler was hanged until "halfe dead" and then beheaded.

Were Leisler's actions justified?

Historians have tried to determine whether Leisler was justified in taking over Fort James and later defying Sloughter. Many point out that Leisler was wrong in trying to promote Protestantism at a time when New York was occupied by many diverse religious groups. He was unduly influenced by his strong Calvinist upbringing, and his religious fervor led him to misread the letter from William III. He had incorrectly assumed that the Protestant king would unconditionally support all Protestant efforts. Nevertheless, even though Leisler was executed, his legacy lived on with the emergence of the Leislerians. These followers of Leisler managed to have the verdict against their leader overturned in 1695. Aside from this achievement, the Leislerians had difficulty gaining political power. The situation changed, however, when they were invited to join the council by Richard Coote, Earl of Bellomont, who became governor in 1698.

For further research

The Leisler Papers Project. http://pages.nyu.edu/_dwvl/ Available July 13, 1999.

McCormick, Charles Howard. *Leisler's Rebellion.* New York: Garland Publishers, 1989.

Reich, Jerome R. *Leisler's Rebellion.* Chicago: University of Chicago Press, 1953.

Index

Italic type indicates volume numbers.

Bold type indicates main entries and their page numbers.

Illustrations are marked by (ill).

H

R

Rackham, Calico Jack *1:* 172
Raleigh, Walter *1:* 26
Read, Mary *1:* 172
Reed, Deborah *1:* 132
Rensselaerswyck *2:* 348
Revolutionary War *2:* 255
Rhode Island *2:* 215
Richelieu, Armand Jean du Plessis *1:* 53
Right Thoughts in Sad Hours 2: 335
Roberval, Jean-François de La Rocque *1:* 46-47
Robinson, William *1:* 90, 111
Rolfe, John *2:* 263-65, **282-89,** 283 (ill.), 288 (ill.)
Roman Catholic Church *2:* 227
Roman Catholic Inquisition *1:* 194
Roman Catholicism *1:* 30, 31, 33, 110, 133, 174; *2:* 273
Rowlandson, Joseph *2:* 291
Rowlandson, Mary White *2:* **290-97,** 290 (ill.), 292 (ill.)
Royal Society *1:* 37

S

Sacred History 1: 137
Saint Augustine *2:* 319
Salem witch trials *2:* 300 (ill.)
San Diego de Alcala Mission *1:* 136 (ill.)
Sandys, Sir Edwin *1:* 158
Santa Maria 1: 60, 62
Secret History 1: 41
The Selling of Joseph 2: 303
Senecas *1:* 81, 83-84; *2:* 268, 270
Separatists *1:* 109; *2:* 373
"Seven Cities of Cibola" *1:* 68-70; 119, 122-24
Seven Years' War *1:* 113
Sewall, Samuel *2:* **298-04,** 298 (ill.), 307
Shawnees *1:* 86; *2:* 268, 271
Shippen, Edward *1:* 82
Sibbes, Richard *1:* 77
Silk winding *2:* 255 (ill.)
"Sinners in the Hands of an Angry God" *1:* 94, 97-98
Slavery *1:* 115 (ill.), 156 (ill.); *2:* 380, 382

Sloane, Hans *1:* 10
Sloughter, Henry *1:* 197-98
Smallpox inoculation *2:* 211
Smibert, John *2:* **305-08,** 305 (ill.)
Smith, John *1:* 54, 139; *2:* 257, 258 (ill.), 262, 279, 284, 286, **309-16,** 309 (ill.), 315 (ill.)
Soto, Hernando de *2:* **317-22,** 317 (ill.), 321 (ill.)
Southwell, Robert *1:* 37
Southworth, Alice Carpenter *1:* 16
Spiritual Milk for Boston Babes in Either England 1: 79, 79 (ill.)
Spotswood, Alexander *1:* 35, 38-39, 38 (ill.)
Squanto *2:* 200-02, **323-28,** 323 (ill.), 326 (ill.)
Standish, Miles *1:* 16, 18-19; *2:* 222
Static electricity *1:* 128
Stephenson, Marmaduke *1:* 90, 111
St. Mark's Episcopal Church *2:* 334
Stoddard, Solomon *1:* 95-97
Stone, John *1:* 110
Strachey, William *2:* 260
Stuyvesant, Peter *2:* **329-34,** 329 (ill.), 351, 385
"Stuyvesant's Bad Government" *2:* 331
Sulpicians *1:* 185
Susquehannocks *1:* 3

T

Tainos *1:* 61
Taylor, Edward *2:* 335-39
Tekakwitha, Catherine (Kateri) *2:* **340-46,** 340 (ill.)
Temple, Thomas *1:* 91
Tennent, Gilbert *2:* 361, 361 (ill.)
The Tenth Muse 1: 21, 24, 25 (ill.), 26
Thanksgiving *1:* 17; *2:* 202
Thirty Years War *1:* 194
Tidewater *1:* 155
"Tiguex War" *1:* 72
Tobacco plantation *2:* 284 (ill.)
Tolerance Act *2:* 247
Tonti, Henry de *1:* 186-87, 190
Tostee, Peter *1:* 82